F-14 TOMCAT

in action

by Lou Drendel

squadron/signal publications

[Cover] F-14A Tomcat of VF-84 fires a Phoenix Missile, as contrails of two other Phoenix streak upward. Phoenix flight profile will take it high above it's target, before final guidance brings it down on it's quarry.

ISBN 0-89747-031-1

Photo Credits

US Navy	S. Ohtaki
Grumman	Scott Brown
Lou Drendel	Bruce Trombecky
Tom Hayden	Hans Redemann
Jim Sullivan	Bob Lawson
Ken Buchanan	Don Logan
Duane Kasulka	
Dr. C. Eddy	

If you have any photographs of the aircraft, armor, soldiers or ships of any nation, particularly wartime snapshots, why not share them with us and help make Squadron/Signal's books all the more interesting and complete in the future. Any photograph sent to us will be copied and the original returned. The donor will be fully credited for any photos used. Please send them to: Squadron/Signal Publications, Inc., 1115 Crowley Dr., Carrollton, TX 75011-5010.

Acknowledgements

As usual, this book, like all of my "In Action" titles, could not have come to fruition without the generous support of many photographers and private collectors. They are credited under their photos. Several other people deserve recognition for their efforts in my behalf, principal among them Captain Dan Macintyre, USNR, whose tireless championing of my cause resulted in my F-14 orientation flight. At Oceana NAS, Captains John Disher, Joe Muka, and Harry Post gave unstinting support to my efforts, and LCDR Dick Schram and his wife, Sharon, made me welcome in their home during my stay in Virginia Beach. My deepest gratitude to all of them, and to the dozens of other people who have helped to make my task a little easier in the compilation of this book.

Variable Sweep Is for the Birds!

Ages and ages ago, Mother Nature outfitted birds with variable sweep wings. Ever since, birds have made good use of these wings, extending them for quick turns, energy-conserving gliding and short landings... sweeping them rearward for high speed diving, and other fancy wingwork. All in all, the variable sweep bird seems to have been a pretty solid design as there's never been a need for product improvements or model changes.

Was it something she just lucked into? Was it the result of extensive research and prototyping? Or was it just the natural thing to do?

We're sure it was the latter but how could we verify it? We found that if the run-of-the-mill, everyday bird had been equipped with a fixed wing, most or all of the following would be true of his characteristics:

* he would be heavier
* he would need more food
* he wouldn't turn as well
* he wouldn't be able to go as far
* he would land faster
* he would need a bigger nest
* he would cost more (if it were possible to cost account a bird)

We must admit that when it comes down to our variable sweep wing capabilities, TOMCAT is really a "Copycat" ...We just hope that Mother Nature understands that copying is the sincerest form of flattery.

We agree. Variable Sweep is for the birds...Naturally!

Grumman Aerospace Corporation

Introduction

"The F-14 Tomcat is the ultimate air-combat weapons system."....So goes the opening line of the Grumman Aerospace Corporation's information sheet on the Tomcat. Parochial as it may seem, this is a fair assessment of the F-14, for the Tomcat has bridged the gap from yesterday to tommorrow, in aerodynamics and avionics.

Even before the Tomcat flew, it was in a battle for survival, as the full wrath of anti-military congressional critics was directed at each new weapons system proposed in the waning months of the Vietnam War. That it was born of the abortive F-111B, which was to have been the Navy version of the F-111A, ne TFX, did nothing to smooth the bumpy road from design to fleet introduction.

The Navy was never convinced that the F-111B could fulfill the fleet air defense assignment, but then Secretary of Defense Robert McNamara insisted upon concurrent development of both A and B versions of the F-111, citing the illusory benefits of "commonality"....an airplane for all seasons, services, and missions. The F-111B was built, rolling out of Grumman's factory in 1965. What had been evident on paper was proven conclusively during testing of the F-111B. It was simply not suitable for carrier operations. It was too heavy. (70,000 lbs. versus the max of 50,000 the Navy had specified for the airplane it wanted.) It was not maneuverable enough. (The Vietnam War had proven that interceptors could be forced into an air superiority situation.) Angles of attack for coming aboard made it almost impossible to see the carrier, and all that extra weight taxed the existing arrester gear to the breaking point. It was patently obvious to the Navy, if not to McNamara and his "whiz kids", that the F-111B was a dead end. When McNamara left DOD, the Navy promptly funded money to Grumman for advanced fighter studies, hoping to come up with a design that could replace the F-111B when the time came.

The time came in May, 1968, when Congress refused to come up with more money for the F-111B program. By that time, the Navy had in hand two proposals from Grumman, designated VFX-1 and VFX-2. The first was to utilize the TF-30 engines of the F-111, while the second would use the Advanced Technology Engine, which was being developed jointly by the USAF and Navy. Both designs included the AWG-9 weapons system, which had been developed by Hughes Aircraft for use in the F-111B. The AWG-9/Phoenix Missile System was to prove the most beneficial aspect of the F-111B program. The Navy had helped Congress to make up it's mind on the F-111B program by institution of their "Navy Fighter Study II", which compared the VFX with the F-111B. The results of that study erased any doubts about the workability of commonality.

In July, 1968, the Navy tendered Request for Proposals to the American aircraft industry. Designs were received from North American Rockwell, LTV, General Dynamics. McDonnell Douglas, and Grumman, with the latter two being chosen as the best. Grumman was announced as the winner of the

Full size engineering mockup of the F-14A, as unveiled by Grumman in early 1969. [Grumman]

design competition in January 1969, and a contract for development of the VFX was signed the following month.

Grumman had taken advantage of all of the lessons learned from current state-of-the-art technology in designing the F-14. They had never seriously considered anything but the swing-wing design, (Only one of six potential designs considered for the VFX had a fixed wing.) and their experience with the F-10F and F-111B programs gave them the solid foundation to build a reliable swing-wing airplane. They used a larger percentage of Titanium than had ever been used in an airplane of this type before. (24% versus only 9% in the F-4) They pioneered the electron-beam welding process which allowed the use of such liberal amounts of Titanium, a metal that is much stronger and lighter than steel. And they had the, by now, well developed AWG-9 weapons system, and the space-age solid state computer to build around. Finally, they were building a pure air-combat weapons system, whose integrity need not be compromised with the addition of a mud-moving mission. The first Tomcat made it's maiden flight on 21 December, 1970. It crashed on it's second flight, on 30 December, but the cause of the crash was known and corrected before the second F-14 flew on 24 May, 1971. This was followed the same year by first flights of the number 9, 4, 5, & 6 airplanes, and the commencement of NPE I.

Mockup demonstrated Grumman's contention that much of on-board maintenance could be accomplished without removal of components, through design and placement of access panels. Forward avionics bay and General Electric M-61 20mm cannon are exposed in this photo. [Grumman]

80% of on-aircraft engine accessory corrective maintenance can be accomplished with engine compartment clamshell door open. [Grumman]

Easy access to AWG-9 radar is demonstrated in shot of fold-up radome. Also note extended refueling probe. [Grumman]

Airbrake Mechanism

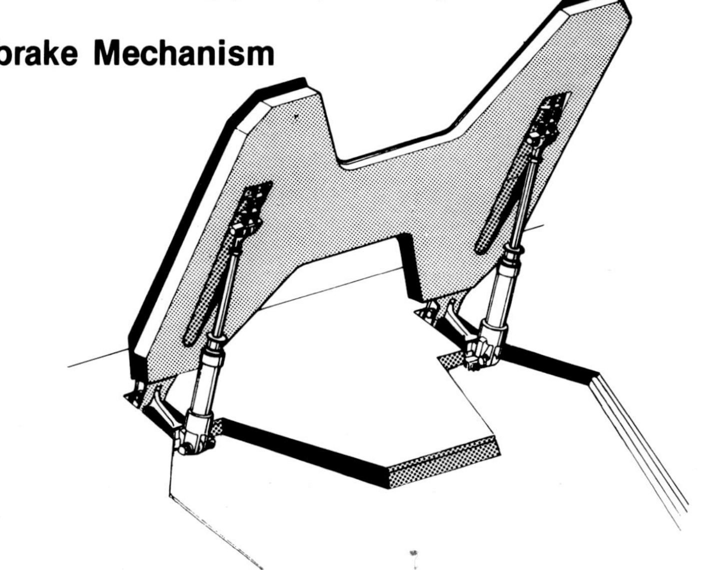

Accompanied by A-6 chase plane, F-14 number 2 returns to Calverton after its first flight, on May 24, 1971. It was designated as the low-speed, high lift and stall/spin test aircraft. Wings were locked in 20 degree sweep position, and variable engine air inlet was locked full open for these tests. [Grumman]

Aircraft number three was devoted to structural buildup and demonstration. It was to test G-loadings for 6.5 for air-to-air, and 7.5 for ground attack missions. First flight was December 28, 1971. [Grumman]

George W. White, Jr. [left] and Emory Brown aboard USS Forrestal [CVA-59] during carrier trials of the F-14, in June 1972. White was first Naval Aviator to fly the Tomcat, Brown the fourth, and the first to fly it off of and on to a carrier. [US Navy]

Tomcat Testing

LCDR Emory Brown has over 4,000 hours of fighter flight time, with 750 hours in the F-14, including a cruise with VF-142 aboard USS America. His experience includes combat tours flying the F-4, with VF-11 and VF-102. He is a graduate of U.S. Navy Test Pilot School, and he served with the Carrier Suitability Branch of Flight Test at NATC Patuxent River, where he was F-14 OPEVAL Project Manager. He was the fourth Navy pilot to fly the F-14, and conducted the initial carrier trials in the F-14 test program. He is scheduled to command VF-41 "Black Aces". These are his impressions of the Tomcat:

"One of the primary lessons taught at Test Pilot School was avoidance of emotional involvement in a test project. We learned that lesson well, and I assure you that the precept was retained for at least two days following assignment of the F-14 carrier suitability project. The sudden responsibility of ensuring accurate and complete testing, objective analysis, and acceptance or rejection of design features of the next generation Navy fighter fell on the shoulders of a few test pilots and project engineers. Emotional involvement?...You bet!! We lived F-14 for three years of program monitor and flight testing. They were complex years, made up of frustration, extraordinary satisfaction, highs, lows, politics, professional accomplishment, physical and emotional fatigue, and the best flying this side of combat.

The product does not have **all** of the flying qualities for **all** of the capabilities that we as test-pilots-soon-to-be-returned-to-fleet-operational-flying would have desired. **But,** it is unquestionably a superior weapons system and a mean flying machine. I feel a tremendous sense of accomplishment and pleasure in recalling my professional association with the development of the Tomcat.

I joined the F-14 Evaluation Team immediately upon graduation from TPS, while the program was still in a monitor status, and remained with it until the beginning of BIS trials. (Board of Inspection and Survey, which is the last step in Navy evaluation of a new aircraft before it is accepted into

Aircraft number 2 as it appeared late in test program, loaded with six Phoenix, two Sidewinder missiles, and aux fuel tanks. Spin-stabilizing drogue chute housing is visible on beaver-tail between engines. [Fitted for the test program only.] [Grumman]

NPE team poses with aircraft number 15, first of a block of four airplanes assigned for pilot training. [Grumman]

the fleet.) CDR George White was the team leader and the flying qualities and performance specialist. The team that I will be referring to consisted of six pilots, two each from carrier suit and flying qualities and performance, (Flight Test) and two from the fighter branch of Service Test, whose specialty was engines.

My partner was LCDR (now CDR) Gene Tucker, a superb fighter pilot and a totally dedicated and professional test pilot. Gene and I had been in combat in sister squadrons, where we developed a strong friendship and mutual respect. During the initial evaluation of the airplane we found that our previous association and sense of loyalty was the key element in a fight that essentially posed Carrier Suit against the Fleet, Grumman, The Naval Air Systems Command, and other members of the evaluation team. Sounds like heavy odds, doesn't it! The object that generated this massive hassle was DLC (Direct Lift Control), a concept that had been partially tested in an F-8, but first incorporated in the F-14 as a production feature. More about DLC later.

The first Navy Preliminary Evaluation (NPE 1) followed a year of monitor during which we practically commuted between Patuxent River and the Grumman plant on Long Island. During this period, The NPE team and Bill Miller (F-14 Project pilot for Grumman, and probably the most significant contributor to the excellence of the airplane), became deeply involved in training on airplane systems and analysis of contractor test flight results. We began to sense areas that required a closer look, and to develop our flight test plans accordingly. We also became acquainted with a totally new concept in data acquisition, which was to revolutionize flight testing. The ATS (Automated Telemetry System) was designed to monitor airplane system and engine parameters and flight data in real time, which enabled the pilot to concentrate with precision on his particular test, while the ATS specialist monitored operating limits. An immediate readout permitted immediate repetition of the test if required, and validated results of a good test. It's almost impossible to stress too much the importance of ATS to the F-14 program.

NPE 1 provided us with our first opportunity to fly the airplane. The psychological and emotional factors that a test pilot experiences on first flight and the personal pressures that follow cover a wide spectrum. The sheer excitement of strapping on the most advanced tactical fighter aircraft in the world, flying it from first roll to liftoff in 1200 feet, rotating immediately to 70 degrees nose up, then looking over your shoulder as you pass through 15,000 feet and seeing that you are still within the airport boundaries....well, that's exhiliarating! But the return to reality and objective analysis must be immediate, as the test plan permits only eight carrier suitability flights during NPE 1. I had to stifle the urge to leave her in zone five afterburner and recite "High Flight" over and over and over again. At that moment, there is no man in the world who I would trade jobs with.

My immediate reaction, from a technical standpoint, was that of a tight, responsive control system, tremendous power, and an exceptionally honest airplane. The high Alpha (angle of attack) characteristics were most impressive, and the controllability afforded by the two large vertical tails and rudders was remarkable. The F-14 is a true rudder airplane that will perform unbelievable best moves in the hands of a fighter pilot. The human engineering that Grumman designed into both cockpits is a work of art, with all controls lying within easy reach. I was so totally impressed with the machine in my hands that I became concerned about my ability to remain objective. But that quickly passed as the test plan prosecution began. The hot mike interchange with ATS, during which every comment was taped with the data, tends to tone down ICS commentary and remind the pilot of his primary mission.

I was to devote a majority of my flight time during NPE 1 to the power approach (landing) configuration, and on one flight actually conducted 92 field carrier landing practice approaches. We air-refueled twice during that test flight, a practice which had a similar revolutionary effect on flight testing as that of ATS. That particular flight was a 5.7 hour endurance test...an unbelievably long time for a fighter pilot with a 2.1 hour tail. We looked at every imaginable combination of flap, wing sweep, speed brake, auto-throttle, and DLC configurations with capability to correct to glideslope from all potential error situations that a carrier pilot might experience. We flew from high, fast starts, and low, slow starts to settles at the ramp, and climbs at the ramp, and evaluated airplane response to corrections. We found some interesting results, particularly considering that the airplane was advertised to be better at the back end of the boat than anything in the inventory.

Let's talk about DLC now, and I'll discuss the carrier boarding characteristics in light of that subject.

Direct Lift Control is a landing aid, provided by the four individual spoilers on the top of each wing. When DLC is engaged, by pushing a button on the stick, the spoilers pop up to a neutral position. They can be commanded full up (+15 degrees) or full down (-4.5 degrees) with a thumb wheel on the side of the stick. When we became more familiar with it, we discovered that we could make very precise adjustments with DLC, without changing the attitude of the airplane. There is a stabilator input that compensates, of course, since DLC changes your center of pressure, which in turn changes the pitch attitude of the airplane. We use DLC in conjunction

Tomcat approaches field-arrestment gear at Pax River during "Shake, Rattle, and Roll" tests. [US Navy]

Emory Brown and Gene Tucker preflight F-14 at Pax River. Tucker would later earn notoriety by bagging a Mig-21 at night over North Vietnam, while flying a Phantom with VF-103.

Main Landing Gear

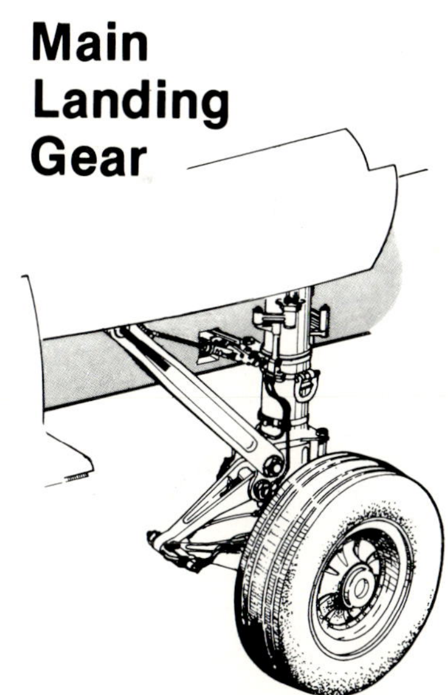

Tomcat on the Independence, during non-flying deck trials to demonstrate it's carrier compatibility for congressional skeptics. It is shown taxiing off elevator and into hangar deck, and taxiing on deck under watchful eyes of deck crew, who were ever-ready with chocks in hand. [US Navy]

with auto-throttle, and the combination is really very nice for flying aboard.

Throughout the test program, Grumman was under the Congressional gun, and under public scrutiny for potential cost overruns and all the other buzz words that apply to the typical defense contractor today. (Authors note:) It should be remembered that Grumman was laboring under a fixed-cost contract that, because of inflation, would eventually bring the company to the brink of bankruptcy. Government negotiators, also feeling the pressure of the above noted buzz words, were unwilling to relent on the contract.) They were in a tight position, and anticipated even tighter days coming, while trying to function within the letter of the detail specifications for the F-14, in order to avoid costly penalties. One primary requirement called for a maximum carrier landing speed of 128 knots. This is a tight restriction for an airplane capable of speeds in excess of mach 2.4, but Grummans swing-wing design managed to accomplish it...except with DLC engaged. DLC adds 6 knots to the approach speed and, at max arrested landing weight, generated a 132 knot approach speed. There were 2 options as far as Grumman was concerned...Increase the optimum angle of attack for approach by 2 units, thereby slowing the airplane to 128 knots...Or delete DLC.

While furiously lobbying with NAVAIR and The Fleet, and attempting to convince us to accept option two, Grumman installed a complex dual action angle of attack bug that varied optimum approach selection from 15 units in conventional configuration, to 17 units with DLC engaged. The auto-throttle computer responded accordingly. Not a bad idea, you might say. Well, Gene Tucker and I disagreed entirely with the concept and with both of Grumman's options. The airplane flies much better at 15 units AOA, and must have DLC engaged to generate decent engine response and provide the improved flying qualities that accompany a slightly higher airspeed. Those of us who have landed aboard an aircraft carrier on a black, rainy, turbulent night with a very low ceiling, and no divert field in the vicinity, will tell you that the epic "High Flight" does not apply at that instant. What does apply is rapid and effective response from flight controls and engines and a stable flying machine. In deference to those select few of the world's

aviators who would fly the F-14 in those conditions, we insisted on the third option...Retain DLC, consider it mandatory for night and preferable for day operation, give Grumman relief on the specification requirement for 128 knots, and set the optimum approach AOA at 15 units. Sounds logical, and should be simple, right? Well, it wasn't so simple, because Grumman did not believe that they could escape the cost penalty. Thus began **"The Great DLC Fight of the Century"**.

First let's set the record straight on the F-14 in the carrier landing environment. The rigidity of design spec for both high and low speed performance requirement generated some features in the landing configuration that increase pilot workload. With training, the basic airplane (without DLC) can be flown aboard nicely, but honors for the Golden Tailhook (awarded to the squadron whose carrier landing performance is the best within the airwing) are more difficult to achieve than with the F-4. The basic airplane is perfectly safe, it just isn't beautifully smooth on the glide-slope. It has high pitch inertia similar to the RA-5C; float characteristics like the A-6A; residual thrust from the fan engines that keep the throttles in the lower, less responsive zones; a gust responsive wing; side force characteristics that decrease seat of the pants sensitivity to sideslip; a lateral control system (spoilers) that stairstep it with lineup corrections and diminish precise heading control; and an auto-throttle that requires considerable anticipation. These observations are all relative, and I base my analysis on a comparison with all other contemporary fleet aircraft. (Authors note: LCDR Brown is carrier qualified in all tactical Navy aircraft, and has flown all contemporary Navy aircraft. He has taken individual Golden Tailhook honors in two air wings, and is highly respected within the Naval Aviation community.)

Now I am going to hedge a bit and qualify my statements for those skeptics who will read this analysis and interpret it incorrectly. We have addressed the basic airplane flying qualities without DLC engaged. To a test pilot whose responsibility is to dissect and evaluate the airplane, the features discussed are all significant, but the fleet can live with them and perform in a safe environment. Pilot workload is increased by each, but the human being is adaptable and with training and experience will learn to accept them and to

Emory Brown and Phil Anselmo discuss preflight with Grumman plane captain prior to test flight at Calverton. [Grumman]

[Below Right] Number 2 with flaps, slats, landing gear, and speed brakes out. Note large stiffeners on fuselage, inboard of wings. Size of these was cut down on production aircraft. [Grumman]

Another view of the number 2 airplane, showing position of six Phoenix missiles. Wings are in full 68 degree sweep position. [Grumman]

maximize his performance accordingly. The single most significant factor in facilitating pilot adaptation is DLC. The extension of spoilers slightly into the airstream increases drag, which improves flying qualities laterally and longitudinally and thereby reduces the glideslope and lineup problems. Auto-throttle capability is improved with all these factors...and the attorney for the defense rests his case!

There are still scars all over my body from the DLC Caper, but it **is** in production airplanes and it **does accomplish** design tasks. Without DLC we would have some real problems flying the F-14 aboard the boat.

After the NPE, we had to take the airplane down to Norfolk and hoist her aboard the USS Independence for deck trials. This was fairly significant, because with Congress looking at the airplane for a possible buy or no buy decision, the most important thing is for a carrier airplane to be seen on the deck of a carrier. So we drove it around the deck, up and down the elevators...everything short of flying her, and gave the ship operators an opportunity to become familiar with the F-14. Then we flew her back to Pax River for further contractor demonstrations. They were conducting the carrier arrested landing testing...what we called the "shake", which is short for shake, rattle, and roll. We put the airplane through an awful lot of throes, taking her up to the limits of her design capability, twenty five foot per second landings which the contractor is supposed to demonstrate. During one of these landings, Charlie Brown, the Grumman test pilot, hurt his back very severely. (The airplane came through unscathed.) In flying these tests, I would take the airplane out, for instance, and start with a three degree glide slope, build to 4, 4½, 5 etc., etc., until we got a high sink landing, which was the datum point we were looking for. Then we would take it and fly to what we call a roll and yaw opposite, or a roll and yaw same. If it's a roll and yaw opposite, it's a steady heading sideslip, in which I have 5 degrees right wing down, and five degrees left sideslip, which I hold all the way until

Number 2 F-14 is refuelled by the number four A-6, which is still maintained and flown by Grumman from its Calverton, N.Y. flight test facility. Use of several in-flight refuellings on each flight allowed maximum amount of data to be collected in minimum time during NPE-1. [Grumman]

[Left] Refuelling from C-130. Excellent low-speed handling qualities of the Tomcat make it a "piece of cake" to refuel from complete range of tankers in Navy inventory. Standard technique of flying formation on the tanker, while NFO "talks you into the basket" is used with the F-14. [Grumman]

touchdown. What we achieve from this is substantial side forces on the second wheel to touch down, through the moment arm, and it also has a substantial twist on the airframe. A roll and yaw same entails flying the glidepath and, just before touchdown, applying lateral and directional control inputs. A missed wire (bolter) is really interesting, because the side of the runway is then sitting in the ground roll path. That usually required a quick and delicate response to liftoff without grass in the mainmounts. Then we would fly a 1½ to 2 degree glideslope, which is very flat, to a free flight engagement. As we approach the runway, we start to increase the angle of attack, until we feel the hook dragging on the deck. When it catches the wire, it really slams me back down. Then we fly to an off-center arrested landing, in which we land 20 feet left or 20 feet right of the centerline on a very short runout arresting wire…which is a hell of a rough landing. That's a shake…and that's the kind of a test we put the F-14 through. The concept was to subject the airplane to the most radical landing that might be encountered aboard ship. At the end of these demonstrations, we had about another four months of testing to do before we could actually take the airplane aboard ship.

About that time, the word came down from CNO that there was a lot of talk in Congress about the airplane not being carrier suitable, and there was some talk about scrapping the whole project. All of this talk stemmed from

Plugged into the basket and taking on fuel. Instrumented boom on nose recorded yaw, pitch, and roll data during all phases of flight testing. [Grumman]

some of the official technical language that we used in our reports that were leaked to people like Jack Anderson, who then printed it out of context, or because of their ignorance of the way new aircraft testing is done, drew incorrect conclusions from the wording. For example, we had several categories of deficiencies that we used in grading various aspects of the airplane. A "preclude" deficiency would "Preclude mission accomplishment", a "limit" deficiency would "Limit mission accomplishment", and an "avoid" deficiency would be "avoid in future design", which meant that we could live with it on this airplane, but don't incorporate that feature in the next airplane you design. And of course, topping them all in significance, was the "safety of flight" deficiency. Well, when Congress sights one of these reports, they see that wording and immediately conclude that the airplane is design deficient. The upshot of the whole thing was that Congressional pressure forced us to take the airplane aboard ship four months early, to prove that the F-14 could do what it was designed to do...that is, operated on and off a carrier.

We were forced to give it our best shot right up until the last minute, getting the airplane ready for carrier operations. Then we made thirteen touch and go landings and two arrested landings on the Forrestal, and that was our first experience with the machine. These operations were not without problems. The F-14 has a boosted throttle, which requires about seven pounds of force to actuate. When that fails, it reverts to manual mode, which normally requires fourteen pounds of pressure...and that is very significant! I had to fly the airplane aboard ship that way. We also had a wing sweep problem. The flap rigging was giving us problems, and the wing would stick at 50 degrees. I had to overcome that problem while airborne, so that I could bring the airplane aboard ship. During all of this, there was an F-4 waiting on deck, ready to launch with the films of our tests. As soon as we finished, the film was loaded on the F-4, and flown to Andrews AFB, where the film was offloaded, rushed to Anacostia for processing, and hand carried to CNO, who took it to Congress...just to prove to the people on the hill we had successfully operated the F-14 off and on a carrier. It was a shame that we were put through all of that...they knew the airplane was good, and the pressure on us was terrific. During that period...I believe it was from the 9th of March until the end of August...we worked from 6 a.m. until 10 p.m....every day...without a day off...Saturday, Sunday, 4th of July...or anything! That encompassed deck trials, then to carrier preparations, then to carrier trials. Shortly after we returned from carrier trials, Bill Miller was killed while practicing for an airshow. He was to have done a max performance takeoff, climbing to 2,000 feet, rolling over, and while turning within the field boundaries, sweep the wings from full forward to full aft. During a practice run he encountered the same problem with the wing that I had, with the wing sticking at 50 degrees. We all knew about the problem, and knew that it could be corrected by "tricking" a flap interlock microswitch that wasn't being met. This was one of those days when there is fairly low ceiling, which sort of obscures the horizon. Bill had flown out over the bay and, apparently, while he was looking down in the cockpit, trying to trick this switch, he flew into the water. The cost of this crash to the program was immeasurable, mostly because of the loss of Bill Miller, but also because the airplane was highly instrumented for our tests. It was the only airplane we had instrumented for carrier suit at the time. The

situation was sensitive, and we had to recover the airplane to prove what had happened, though there was absolutely no doubt in my mind what we would find.

As we concluded the accident investigation, we progressed immediately into NPE 2, for a look at the discrepancy corrections from NPE 1, and a significantly expanded flight envelope. I really had the opportunity to look at the F-14 as a fighter in the typical ACM environment during this evaluation as we were able to complete the carrier suit evals and delve into the flying qualities and performance side the house. My technical analysis... "OUT OF SIGHT!" My objective analysis... "FAR OUT!!" I hauled that airplane through a series of overheads, high-G turns, and slow speed maneuvers that would have departed and spit out anything else in the air and flew her straight up until she hit zero and backed down and then did it all over again. I had achieved total confidence in this machine with a minimal amount of experience and felt like I had put her on like a tight fitting jumpsuit, rather than stepped in and sat down. Do I sound like a Tomcat Advocate? Well, I have had ample justification and opportunity to become one. There is no airplane better for the multiple mission. In fact, there are none that even come close! I want to elaborate on that, but first let me cover one more subject that I consider to be very important.

We didn't anticipate an active spin problem and the Grumman approach

Emory Brown discussing a point during NPE. Fatigue is evident on faces of all pilots, as they worked a five month stretch of 16 hour days, without a single day off, in order to head off critics of the F-14 who kept constant pressure on for cancellation of the program. In spite of all the flak thrown at it, and the killing pace maintained throughout the test program, the Tomcat proved itself one of the safest airplanes ever to enter the fleet. [Grumman]

The number fourteen airplane being hoisted aboard carrier. It was used for maintenance and reliability work in the test program. [US Navy]

Number ten airplane was used for initial carrier qualifications of the Tomcat. It is seen on number one cat of USS Forrestal during June, 1972 tests. Tremendous heat generated by F-14's twin TF-30 engines requires use of new, water cooled, Mark 7 blast deflectors on carriers operating the F-14. Forrestal had just had the new deflectors installed at time of these tests. [US Navy]

to analysis was that of spin prevention, rather than spin recovery investigation. Chuck Sewell, Chief Test Pilot for Grumman, had the number two airplane specially instrumented and equipped for his spin program. The airplane had a large spin chute, a hydrozine APU for engine restart, and canards fitted alongside the nose. Chuck is a wizard in the flight test game, and was honored for his accomplishments in the F-14 program. We lost the advanced analysis of the spin testing when a hydrozine leak atomized and caught fire during flight. Chuck brought her home, but the bird received strike damage and was not to fly again. As a result of his tests, however, a spin prevention device was developed for the airplane that took conventional lateral control surfaces out of pilot control and shifted roll to rudders in response to stick input at high alpha. An interesting approach that we are still evaluating.

We have lost three airplanes to spins, but two were in the test environment and resulted from unusual circumstances that occurred at the outer edge of the envelope. The third is still under investigation. NASA testing indicated that the F-14 would spin only in the flat mode, and would be irrecoverable once established, but also that a significant effort and failure to apply proper departure recovery techniques would be required to spin the bird. We in the fleet consider the spins to date to be isolated and do not consider loss of control and spin to be an operational problem.

The F-14 began life as a tremendous concept. Grumman had done their homework during their participation in the F-111 program. So when the time came for the F-14 competitive bids, they were ready. We were pushing the state of the art in a lot of areas...the fan engines for a fighter, with afterburner...the variable geometry wing...the newest concepts in controls and displays...and a subject on which I have not commented, the unparalelled AWG-9 weapons system and Phoenix Missile. The most controversial of these had been the engines. It turns out that we really need the advanced technology engines, both from the higher thrust and better fuel specifics features. We really had some initial problems with our TF-30-P412 engines, but they have been corrected and our confidence level restored. Just as the failure to incorporate new engines as scheduled resulted from a failure of those in power on the hill to recognize our requirements, most other problems with the airplane were a result of the push for fleet introduction and a shortfall of funding. We still operate on a shoestring with insufficient parts to repair our machines. But, that's another story, to be told another day.

When everything is said and done, I am extremely excited about the F-14. The weapons system that we have in it is superb. We can do things with the F-14, in a forced defense environment, that you couldn't do with a dozen F-4s. I feel when I'm up there that I have the entire picture. The radar capability is just fantastic, and the weapons that we carry allow us to engage from 80 miles out, right down to within gun range. The thought that went into designing the airplane, not just as an interceptor, but as a total fighter, was really just fantastic! The ultimate catalyst that makes this airplane superior to the air superiority fighters currently in vogue is the two man concept. The NFO is the most valuable asset that Navy tactical aviation has today. In the intercept role he is a dedicated weapon system operator; In the ACM role, he's another set of eyes, another skilled tactician and a superb protective device. I am completely sold on the Tomcat, and I am looking forward to a long and rewarding relationship with the bird.

Tomcat being positioned on the number one catapult of the USS Enterprise. [CVA-N-65]. Jet blast deflector is 36 feet wide, 14 feet high, and folds flush into carrier deck. [US Navy]

Tomcat number 41 [158980] performing touch-and-goes on the Forrestal, November, 1973. It was performing Carrier Suitability Tests, as the test program continued. Per copy cost of the F-14 at this time was $14.7 million, including R&D, support equipment, and spares. [US Navy]

Nose gear has cleared the catapult shuttle as F-14 begins to rotate from the deck of USS Forrestal. [US Navy]

Number 15 airplane launches from the waist cat of the Enterprise in March, 1974. This launch was accomplished using military power only. [no afterburner] [US Navy]

Tomcat crew completes preflight checks, as RA-5C approaches Forrestal for landing, December, 1973. [US Navy]

Bomb Rack

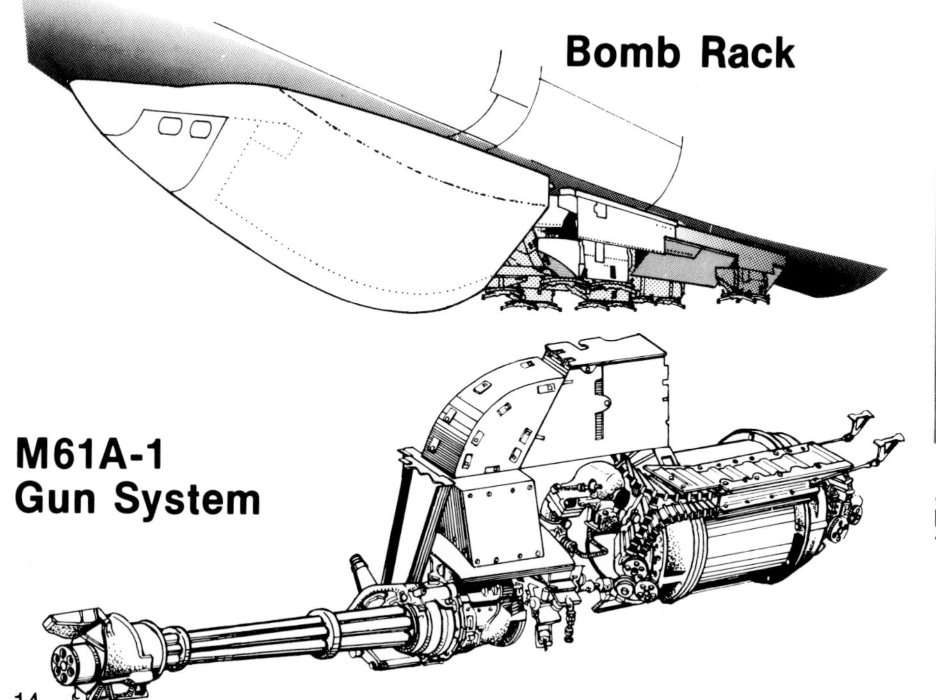

M61A-1
Gun System

Approaching Forrestal for touch and go landing. [Note tailhook is not extended but speed brake is.] In early 1973, the Navy proposed acquisition of a total of 722 F-14s, including 190 for USMC. [US Navy]

Tomcat hits hard during Carrier Suitability testing touch and go landing aboard Forrestal. Note that flaps and leading edge slats are retracted. Aircraft stability and handling for coming aboard was tested in several configurations. [US Navy]

Coming aboard the Enterprise during familiarization for the first fleet squadrons. Former Phantom drivers found they could no longer count on being number one in the air group, as the straight-wing F-14 was tougher with which to get an "O.K. Pass". [US Navy]

Number 14 Tomcat blew a tire while coming aboard Forrestal during December, 1973 Carrler Suit testing, stopping it dead in it's tracks, with tailhook still engaged to arresting gear. [US Navy]

Hangar deck of Forrestal, with two Tomcats aboard for Carrier Suit tests. F-14 in foreground has wings at 75 degree oversweep position, a feature that enhances handling in confined spaces aboard carriers. [US Navy]

General Daniel "Chappie" James, current Commander of NORAD, after a 1974 orientation flight in the Tomcat with Capt. Lewis "Scotty" Lamoreaux, Fighter Air Early Warning Wing, Pacific. It has been suggested that the F-14, as the best interceptor ever built, would make a logical replacement for ADC's ageing F-106 fleet, though intra-service politics make it's choice highly unlikely. [US Navy]

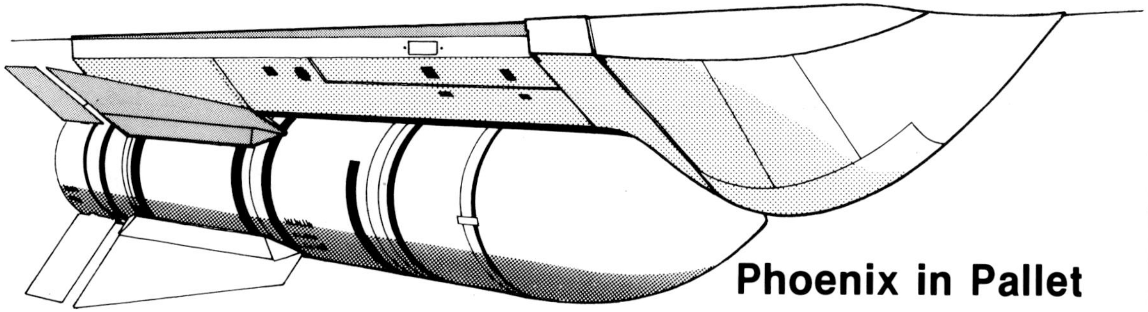

Phoenix in Pallet

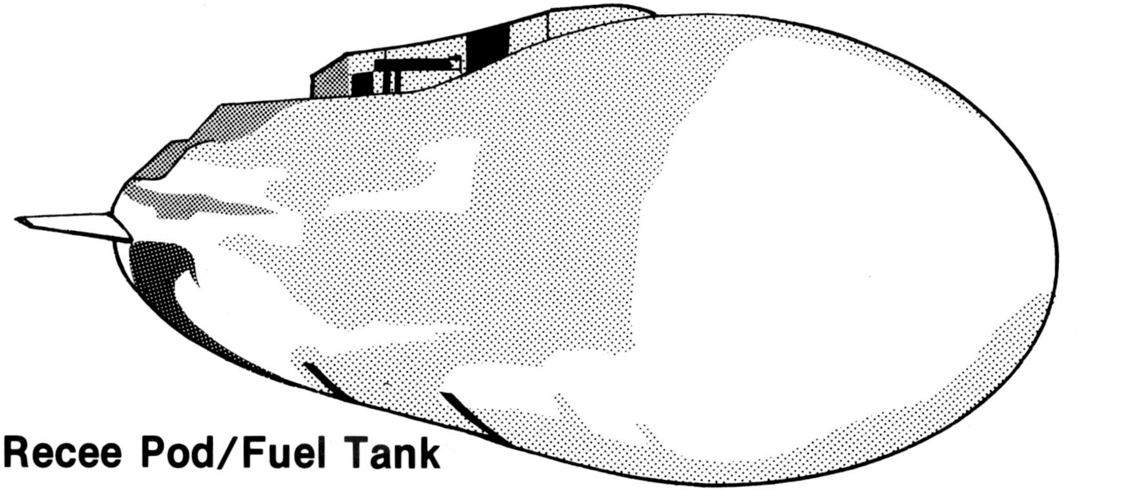

Recee Pod/Fuel Tank

Tomcat vs. Phantom

While the Tomcat was being designed and built, engineers at McDonnell Douglas were striving to find ways to prolong the life of the Phantom. What they came up with was the slatted wing, which dramatically improves the F-4's air combat maneuvering abilities. In fact, the improvement was so dramatic that some insinuations were made to the effect that the slatted Phantom might be able to compete with the Tomcat in the ACM environment. In order to test these theories, the Navy arranged a head-to-head confrontation between the two aircraft. The dogfights took place at Calverton, with Chuck Sewell flying the Tomcat, and Lt. D. Walker, Navy Test Pilot, flying the Phantom.

The initial engagement took place at 35,000 feet at 1.25 mach, with the Tomcat in the lead. Remaining tests ranged down to 18,000 feet at .6 mach.

The Tomcat's performance was superior in all areas. It pulled in excess of 7 Gs in initial breaks, flew at 48 degrees angle of attack, and retained excellent stability and control at speeds as low as 160 knots, while simulating kills on the F-4.

Throughout the test, the Tomcat commanded each engagement, displaying the qualities vital to an air-superiority fighter; maneuverability, turning performance, and specific energy (a measure of excess thrust used to produce superior turn, acceleration, and climb performance.) While in lead position, the Tomcat was out of gun range almost instantly and out of missile launch zone in several seconds....and in a few seconds more, on the tail of the F-4 tracking it!

The major systems which allowed the F-14 to so completely dominate the F-4 were it's afterburning turbofan engines, and it's swinging wings. The wings are automatically positioned by the Mach Sweep Programmer, which provides fully automatic wing sweep as a function of Mach number and altitude. The F-14 also has maneuvering flaps, (the outboard two sections of the landing flaps) which can be extended 10 degrees when the wings are forward of the 50 degree sweep position. The maneuvering flaps are actuated by a thumb-wheel on the stick to increase lift and allow more G to be applied to the airplane, thus enabling it to make tighter turns. Latest models of the F-14 also have leading edge maneuvering slats, which are automatically deployed and retracted at pre-programmed angles of attack.

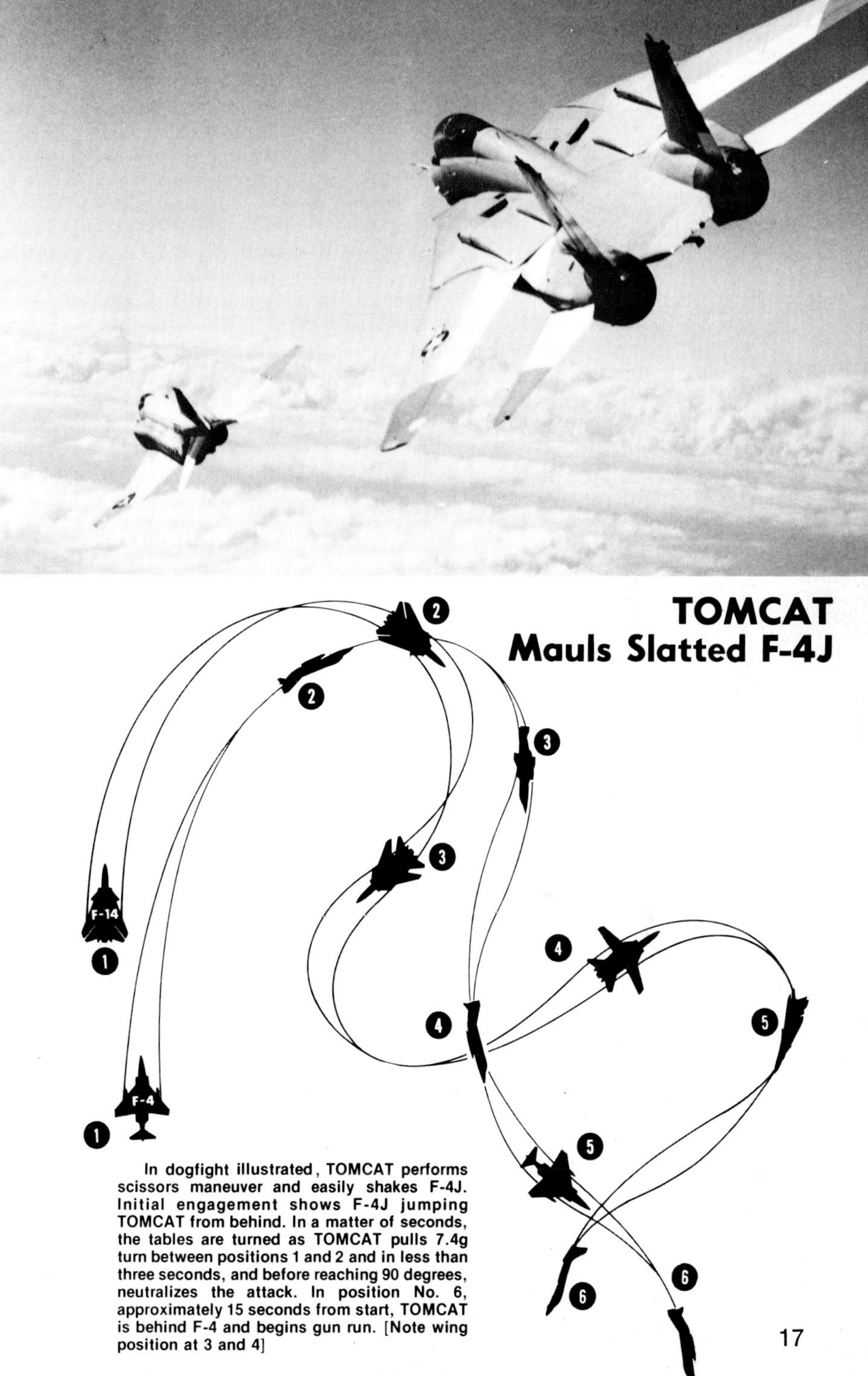

In dogfight illustrated, TOMCAT performs scissors maneuver and easily shakes F-4J. Initial engagement shows F-4J jumping TOMCAT from behind. In a matter of seconds, the tables are turned as TOMCAT pulls 7.4g turn between positions 1 and 2 and in less than three seconds, and before reaching 90 degrees, neutralizes the attack. In position No. 6, approximately 15 seconds from start, TOMCAT is behind F-4 and begins gun run. [Note wing position at 3 and 4]

F-14A

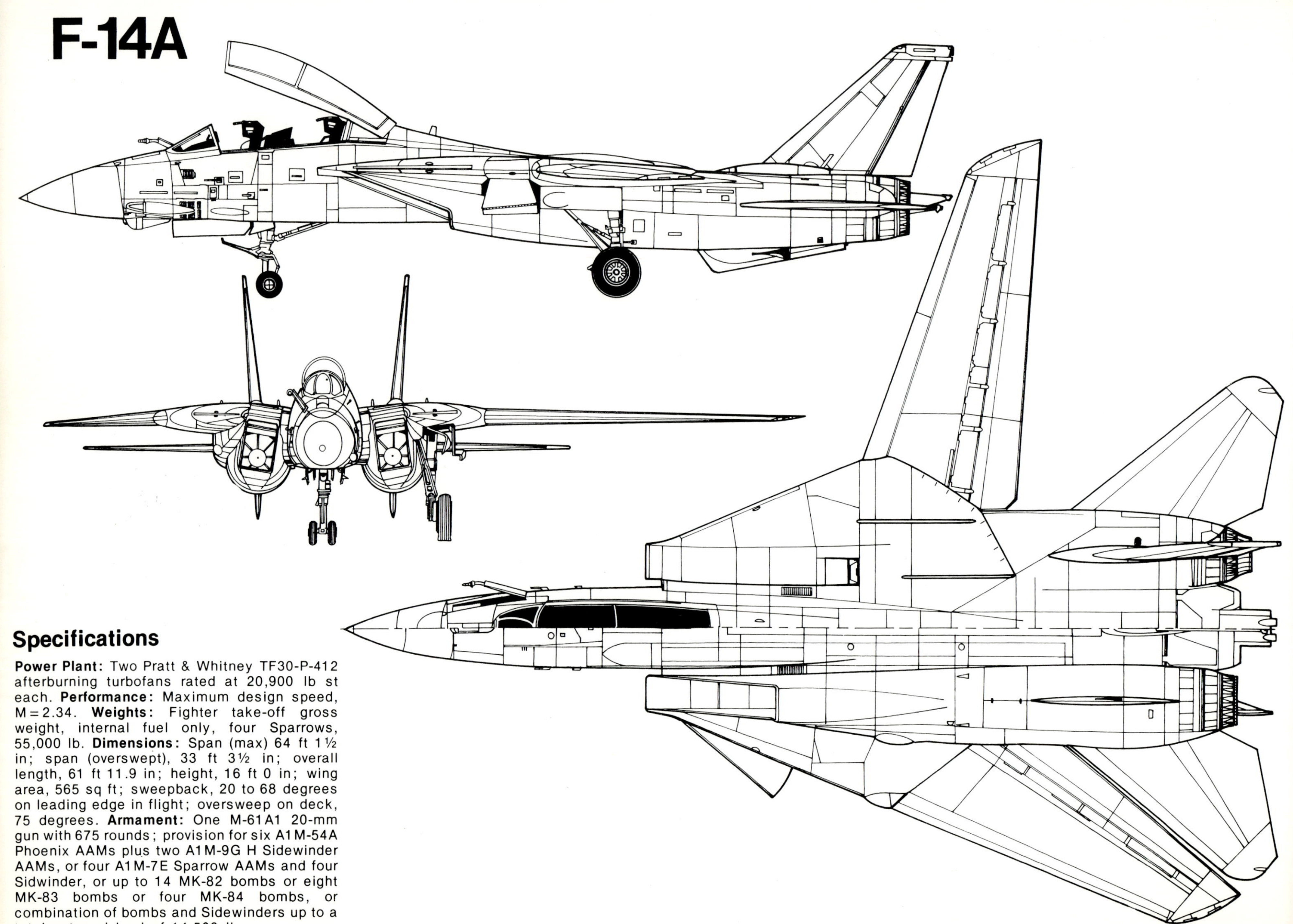

Specifications

Power Plant: Two Pratt & Whitney TF30-P-412 afterburning turbofans rated at 20,900 lb st each. **Performance:** Maximum design speed, M = 2.34. **Weights:** Fighter take-off gross weight, internal fuel only, four Sparrows, 55,000 lb. **Dimensions:** Span (max) 64 ft 1½ in; span (overswept), 33 ft 3½ in; overall length, 61 ft 11.9 in; height, 16 ft 0 in; wing area, 565 sq ft; sweepback, 20 to 68 degrees on leading edge in flight; oversweep on deck, 75 degrees. **Armament:** One M-61A1 20-mm gun with 675 rounds; provision for six A1M-54A Phoenix AAMs plus two A1M-9G H Sidewinder AAMs, or four A1M-7E Sparrow AAMs and four Sidwinder, or up to 14 MK-82 bombs or eight MK-83 bombs or four MK-84 bombs, or combination of bombs and Sidewinders up to a total external load of 14,500 lb.

Wing Control Surfaces

Tomcat Cutaway

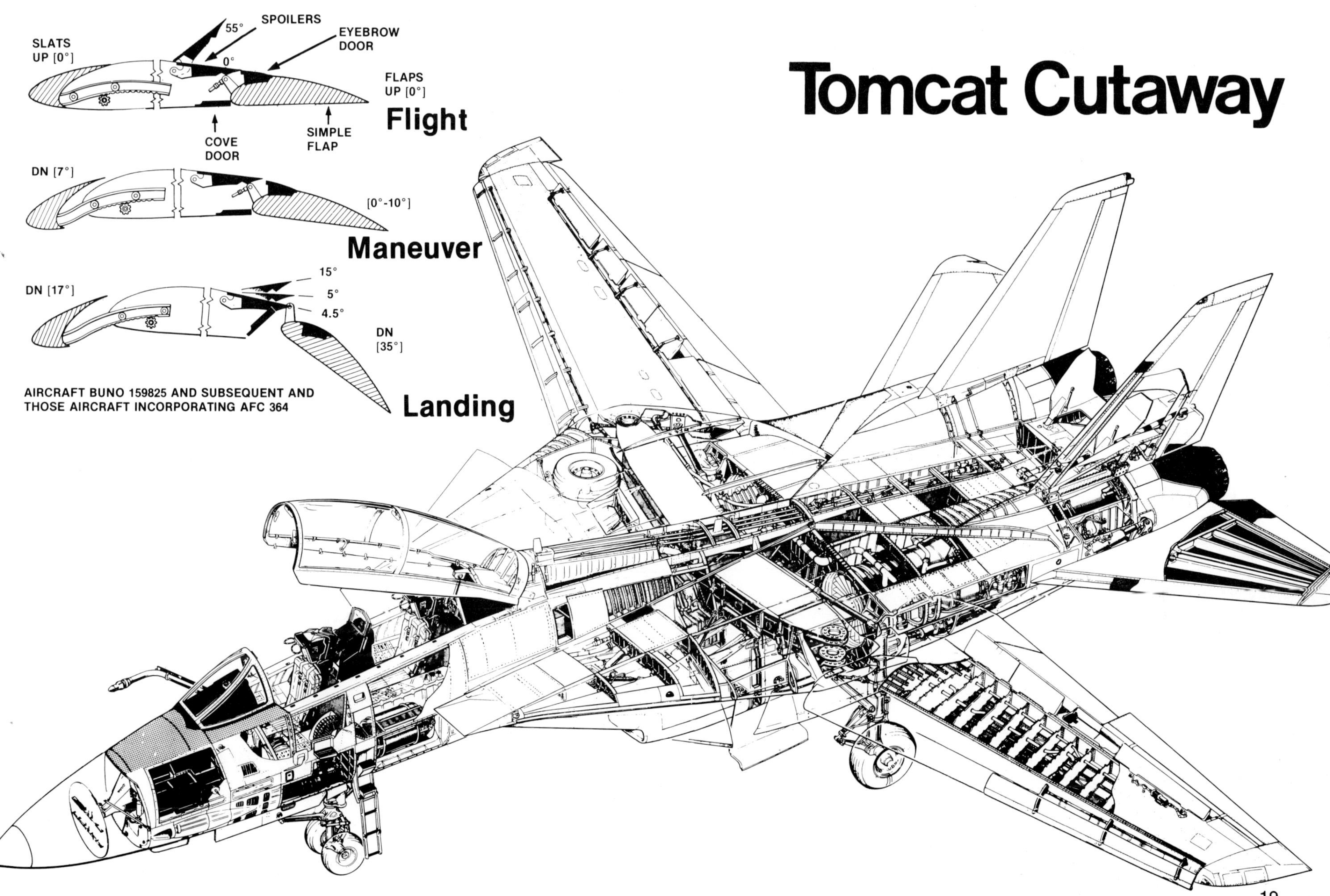

Tomcat Walkaround

[Above Far Left] Nose gear, from front. [Tom Hayden]

[Above Center Left] Phoenix launch pallets, from rear. [US Navy]

[Above Center Right] Tail hook, with safety pin installed. [Tom Hayden]

[Above] Port intake. [Author]

Cranked pylon, with Sidewinder launch rail [top], and Sparrow launch rail [bottom]. [Tom Hayden]

Main gear and wheel well, from front. [Author]

The number 8 airplane was assigned to Pax River for aerodynamic performance and demonstration work of a production configuration aircraft. [Jim Sullivan]

[Right] Boarding ladder, extended. [Author]

[Far Right] Main Gear. [Hans Redemann]

Refueling a pre-production Tomcat aboard Forrestal, during Carrier Suit testing in June, 1972. [US Navy]

Pilot's Instrument Panels

NFO's Instrument Panels

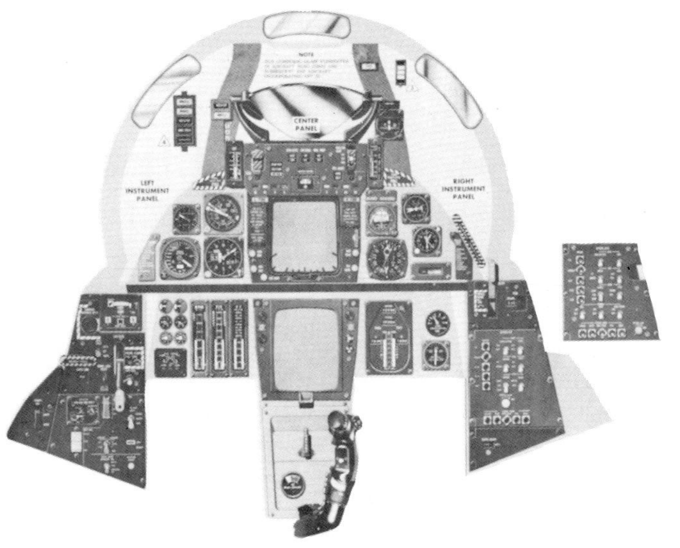

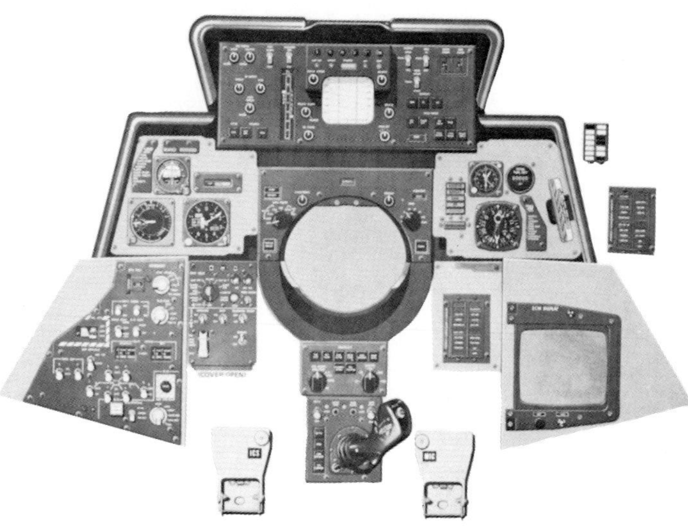

Pilot's Instrument Panel and Consoles

NOTES

1. AIRCRAFT BUNO 158612 THRU 159001
2. AIRCRAFT BUNO 158631 AND SUBSEQUENT AND AIRCRAFT INCORPORATING AFC 35
3. AIRCRAFT BUNO 158978 AND SUBSEQUENT
4. AIRCRAFT BUNO 159002 AND SUBSEQUENT AND AIRCRAFT INCORPORATING AFC 181
5. AIRCRAFT BUNO 159878 AND SUBSEQUENT AND AIRCRAFT INCORPORATING AFC 599
6. AIRCRAFT BUNO 158987 AND SUBSEQUENT AND AIRCRAFT INCORPORATING AFC 529
7. AIRCRAFT BUNO 158978 AND SUBSEQUENT AND AIRCRAFT INCORPORATING AFC 334

LEFT SIDE CONSOLE
1. G VALVE PUSHBUTTON
2. OXYGEN-VENT AIRFLOW CONTROL PANEL
3. COMM/NAV COMMAND CONTROL PANEL
4. INTEGRATED CONTROL PANEL
4a. UHF (AN/ARC 159)
4b. UHF COMM SELECT PANEL
5. TONE VOLUME CONTROL PANEL
6. ICS CONTROL PANEL
7. AFCS CONTROL PANEL
8. THROTTLE QUADRANT
9. INLET RAMPS/THROTTLE CONTROL PANEL
10. TARGET DESIGNATE SWITCH

LEFT VERTICAL CONSOLE
11. FUEL MANAGEMENT PANEL
12. CONTROL SURFACE POSITION INDICATOR
12a. LAUNCH BAR ABORT
13. LANDING GEAR CONTROL PANEL
14. WHEELS-FLAPS POSITION INDICATOR

LEFT KNEE PANEL
15. ENGINE PRESSURE RATIO INDICATOR
16. EXHAUST NOZZLE POSITION INDICATOR
17. OIL PRESSURE INDICATOR
18. HYDRAULIC PRESSURE INDICATOR
19. ELECTRICAL TACHOMETER INDICATOR (RPM)
20. THERMOCOUPLE TEMPERATURE INDICATOR (TIT)
21. RATE OF FLOW INDICATOR (FF)

LEFT INSTRUMENT PANEL
22. SERVOPNEUMATIC ALTIMETER
23. RADAR ALTIMETER
24. AIRSPEED MACH INDICATOR

25. VERTICAL VELOCITY INDICATOR
26. LEFT ENGINE FUEL SHUTOFF HANDLE
27. ANGLE-OF-ATTACK INDICATOR

LEFT FRONT WINDSHIELD FRAME
28. APPROACH INDEXER
29. WHEELS WARNING LIGHT
29a. BRAKES
30. ACLS/AP WARNING LIGHT
30a. NWS ENGA

CENTER PANEL
31. HEADS UP DISPLAY
32. AIR COMBAT MANEUVER PANEL
33. VERTICAL DISPLAY INDICATOR (VDI)
34. HORIZONTAL SITUATION DISPLAY INDICATOR (HSI)
35. PEDAL ADJUST HANDLE
36. BRAKE PRESSURE INDICATOR
37. CONTROL STICK

RIGHT FRONT WINDSHIELD FRAME
38. ECM WARNING LIGHTS
39. STANDBY COMPASS

RIGHT INSTRUMENT PANEL
40. WING SWEEP INDICATOR
41. RIGHT ENGINE FUEL SHUTOFF HANDLE
42. ACCELEROMETER
43. STANDBY ATTITUDE INDICATOR
44. CANOPY JETTISON HANDLE
45. CLOCK
46. BEARING DISTANCE HEADING INDICATOR (BDHI)
47. UHF REMOTE INDICATOR

RIGHT KNEE PANEL
48. FUEL QUANTITY INDICATOR
49. LIQUID OXYGEN QUANTITY INDICATOR
50. CABIN PRESSURE ALTIMETER

RIGHT VERTICAL CONSOLE
51. ARRESTING HOOK PANEL
52. DISPLAYS CONTROL PANEL
53. ELEVATION LEAD PANEL

RIGHT SIDE CONSOLE
54. COMPASS CONTROL PANEL
55. CAUTION—ADVISORY INDICATOR
56. TACAN CONTROL PANEL
57. MASTER GENERATOR CONTROL PANEL
58. ARA-63 CONTROL PANEL
59. AIR CONDITIONING CONTROL PANEL
60. MASTER LIGHT CONTROL PANEL
61. EXTERNAL ENVIRONMENTAL CONTROL PANEL
62. MASTER TEST PANEL
63. HYDRAULIC TRANSFER PUMP SWITCH
64. DEFOG CONTROL LEVER
65. WINDSHIELD DEFOG SWITCH
66. HYDRAULIC HAND PUMP

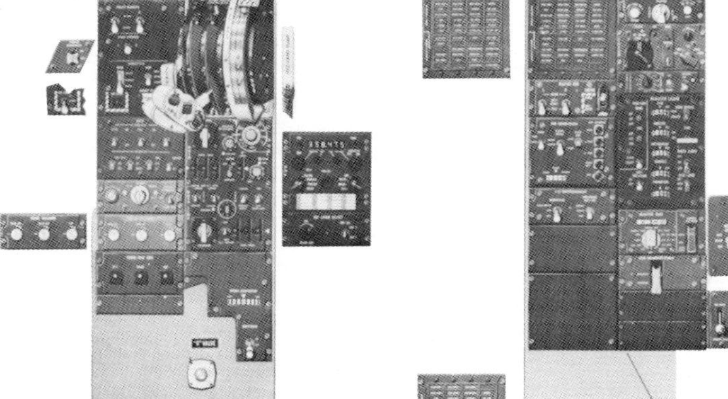

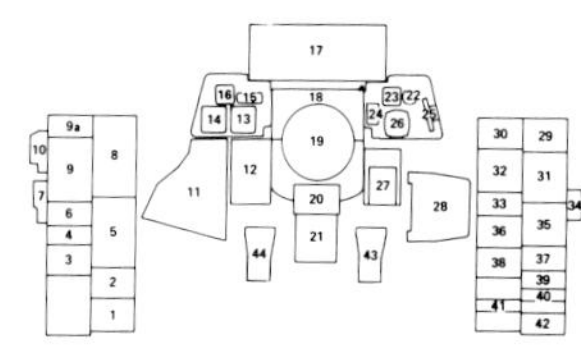

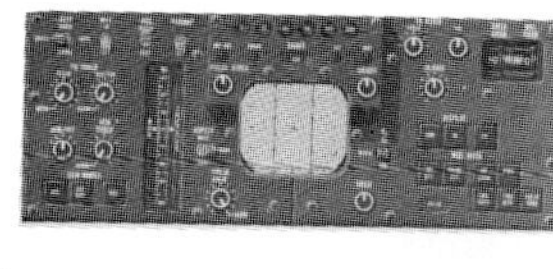

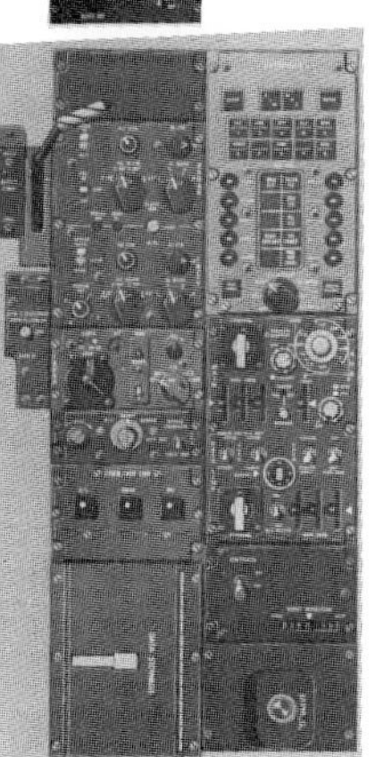

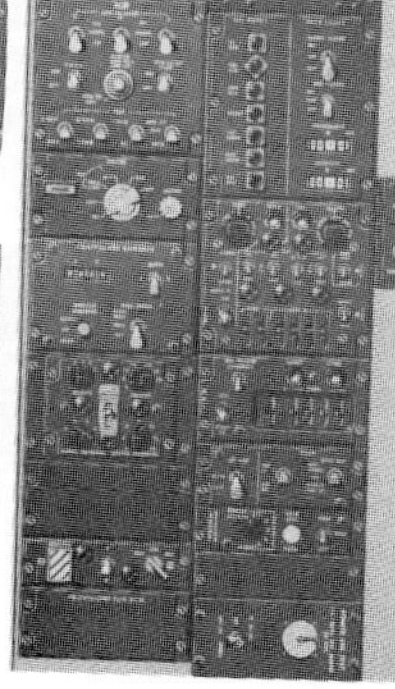

NFO Instrument Panel and Consoles

NOTES

1. AIRCRAFT BUNO 158978 AND SUBSEQUENT
2. AIRCRAFT BUNO 158612 AND SUBSEQUENT
3. AIRCRAFT BUNO 158978 AND SUBSEQUENT AND AIRCRAFT INCORPORATING AFC 599
4. AIRCRAFT BUNO 158978 AND SUBSEQUENT

LEFT SIDE CONSOLE
1. G VALVE PUSHBUTTON
2. OXYGEN-VENT AIRFLOW CONTROL PANEL
3. COMM/NAV COMMAND PANEL
4. ICS CONTROL PANEL
5. INTEGRATED CONTROL PANEL
6. TACAN CONTROL PANEL
7. LIQUID COOLING CONTROL PANEL
8. COMPUTER ADDRESS PANEL
9. RADAR IR/TV CONTROL PANEL
9a. UHF COMM SELECT PANEL
10. EJECT COMMAND PANEL

LEFT VERTICAL CONSOLE
11. ARMAMENT PANEL

LEFT KNEE PANEL
12. SYSTEM TEST — SYSTEM POWER PANEL

LEFT INSTRUMENT PANEL
13. SERVOPNEUMATIC ALTIMETER
14. AIRSPEED MACH INDICATOR
15. UHF REMOTE INDICATOR
16. STANDBY ATTITUDE INDICATOR

CENTER PANEL
17. DETAIL DATA DISPLAY PANEL (DDD)

CENTER CONSOLE
18. NAVIGATION CONTROL AND DATA READOUT
19. TACTICAL INFORMATION DISPLAY (TID)
20. TACTICAL INFORMATION CONTROL PANEL
21. HAND CONTROL UNIT

RIGHT INSTRUMENT PANEL
22. FUEL QUANTITY TOTALIZER
23. CLOCK
24. THREAT ADVISORY LIGHTS
25. CANOPY JETTISON HANDLE
26. BEARING DISTANCE HEADING INDICATOR (BDHI)

RIGHT KNEE PANEL
27. CAUTION-ADVISORY PANEL

RIGHT VERTICAL CONSOLE
28. MULTIPLE DISPLAY INDICATOR

RIGHT SIDE CONSOLE
29. DIGITAL DATA INDICATOR (DDI)
30. ECM DISPLAY CONTROL PANEL
31. DATA LINK REPLY AND INTERIOR LIGHT CONTROL PANEL
32. ECM CONTROL PANEL
33. DECM CONTROL PANEL
34. DEFOG CONTROL LEVER
35. IFF TRANSPONDER CONTROL PANEL
36. CHAFF/FLARE DISPENSE PANEL
37. AA1 CONTROL PANEL
38. AN/ALE-29A PROGRAMMER
39. IFF ANTENNA ANT AND TEST PANEL
40. RADAR BEACON CONTROL PANEL
41. KY-28 CONTROL PANEL
42. ELECTRICAL POWER SYSTEM TEST PANEL

LEFT AND RIGHT FOOT WELLS
43. MIC FOOT BUTTON
44. ICS FOOT BUTTON

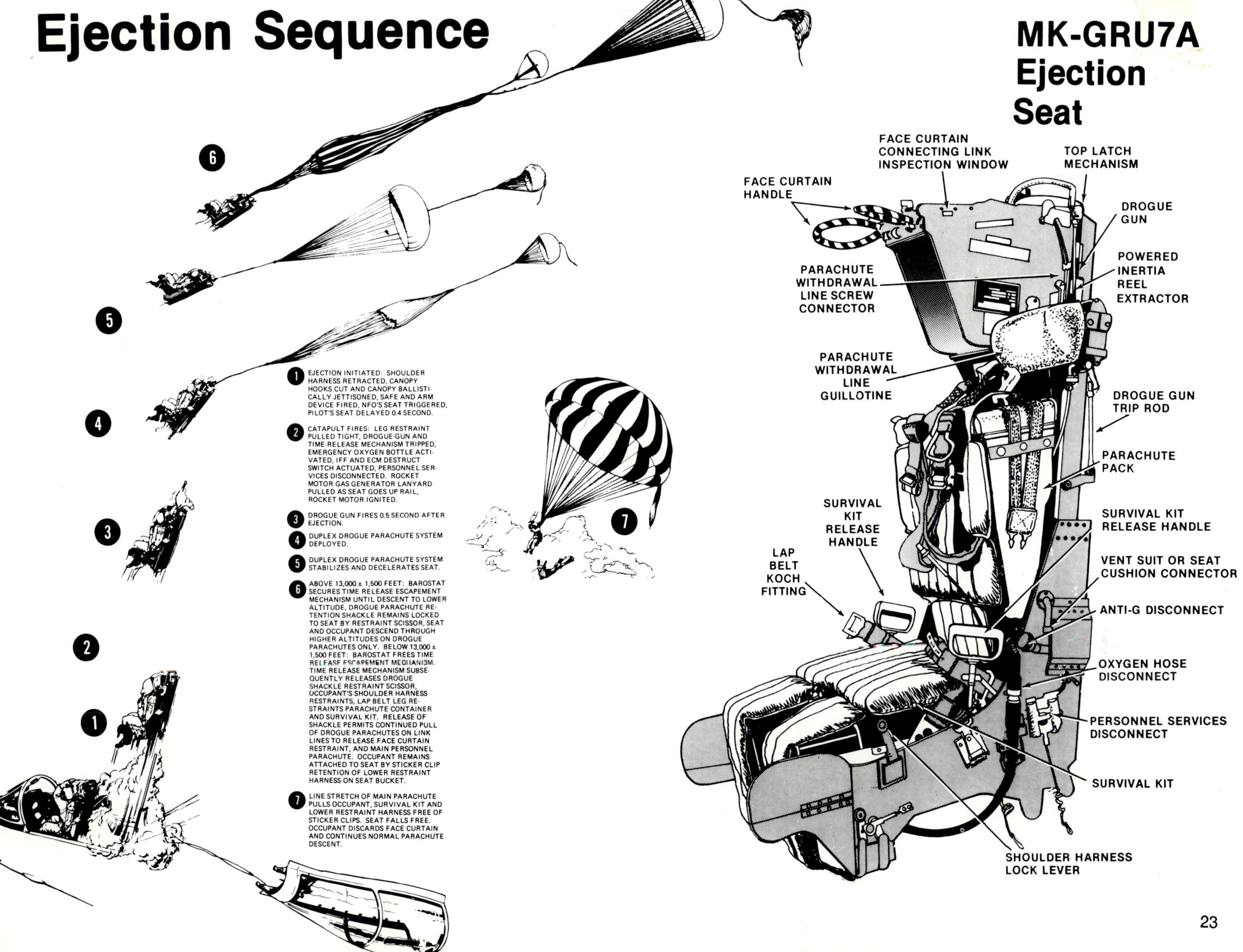

Ejection Sequence
MK-GRU7A Ejection Seat

FACE CURTAIN CONNECTING LINK INSPECTION WINDOW
TOP LATCH MECHANISM
FACE CURTAIN HANDLE
DROGUE GUN
PARACHUTE WITHDRAWAL LINE SCREW CONNECTOR
POWERED INERTIA REEL EXTRACTOR
PARACHUTE WITHDRAWAL LINE GUILLOTINE
DROGUE GUN TRIP ROD
PARACHUTE PACK
SURVIVAL KIT RELEASE HANDLE
SURVIVAL KIT RELEASE HANDLE
VENT SUIT OR SEAT CUSHION CONNECTOR
LAP BELT KOCH FITTING
ANTI-G DISCONNECT
OXYGEN HOSE DISCONNECT
PERSONNEL SERVICES DISCONNECT
SURVIVAL KIT
SHOULDER HARNESS LOCK LEVER

1 EJECTION INITIATED: SHOULDER HARNESS RETRACTED, CANOPY HOOKS CUT AND CANOPY BALLISTICALLY JETTISONED, SAFE AND ARM DEVICE FIRED, NFO'S SEAT TRIGGERED, PILOT'S SEAT DELAYED 0.4 SECOND.

2 CATAPULT FIRES: LEG RESTRAINT PULLED TIGHT, DROGUE-GUN AND TIME-RELEASE MECHANISM TRIPPED, EMERGENCY OXYGEN BOTTLE ACTIVATED, IFF AND ECM DESTRUCT SWITCH ACTUATED, PERSONNEL SERVICES DISCONNECTED. ROCKET MOTOR GAS GENERATOR LANYARD PULLED AS SEAT GOES UP RAIL, ROCKET MOTOR IGNITED.

3 DROGUE GUN FIRES 0.5 SECOND AFTER EJECTION.

4 DUPLEX DROGUE PARACHUTE SYSTEM DEPLOYED.

5 DUPLEX DROGUE PARACHUTE SYSTEM STABILIZES AND DECELERATES SEAT.

6 ABOVE 13,000 ± 1,500 FEET: BAROSTAT SECURES TIME RELEASE ESCAPEMENT MECHANISM UNTIL DESCENT TO LOWER ALTITUDE, DROGUE PARACHUTE RETENTION SHACKLE REMAINS LOCKED TO SEAT BY RESTRAINT SCISSOR, SEAT AND OCCUPANT DESCEND THROUGH HIGHER ALTITUDES ON DROGUE PARACHUTES ONLY. BELOW 13,000 ± 1,500 FEET: BAROSTAT FREES TIME RELEASE ESCAPEMENT MECHANISM. TIME RELEASE MECHANISM SUBSEQUENTLY RELEASES DROGUE SHACKLE RESTRAINT SCISSOR, OCCUPANT'S SHOULDER HARNESS RESTRAINTS, LAP BELT LEG RESTRAINTS PARACHUTE CONTAINER AND SURVIVAL KIT. RELEASE OF SHACKLE PERMITS CONTINUED PULL OF DROGUE PARACHUTES ON LINK LINES TO RELEASE FACE CURTAIN RESTRAINT, AND MAIN PERSONNEL PARACHUTE. OCCUPANT REMAINS ATTACHED TO SEAT BY STICKER CLIP RETENTION OF LOWER RESTRAINT HARNESS ON SEAT BUCKET.

7 LINE STRETCH OF MAIN PARACHUTE PULLS OCCUPANT, SURVIVAL KIT AND LOWER RESTRAINT HARNESS FREE OF STICKER CLIPS. SEAT FALLS FREE. OCCUPANT DISCARDS FACE CURTAIN AND CONTINUES NORMAL PARACHUTE DESCENT.

Weapons Loading

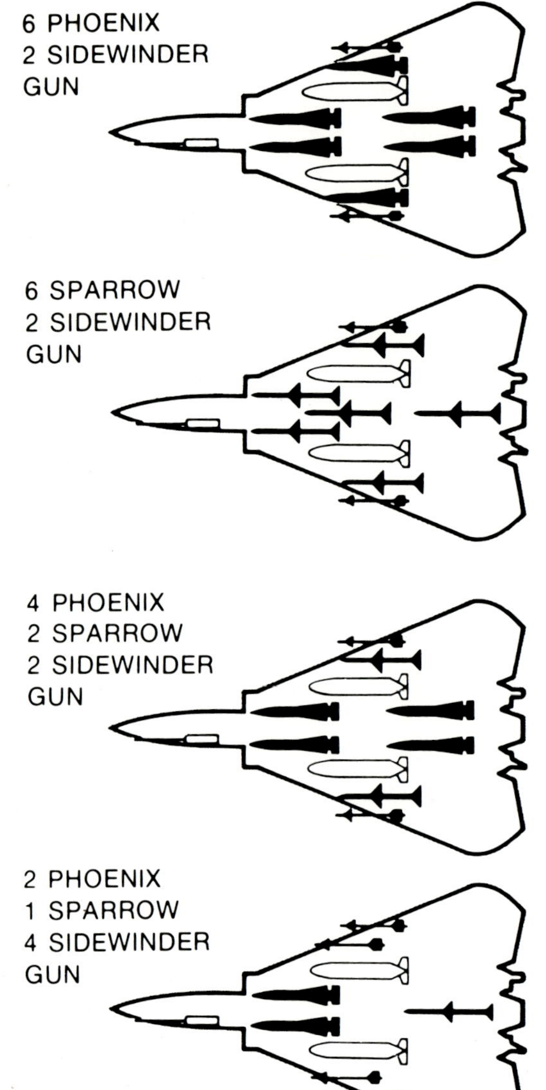

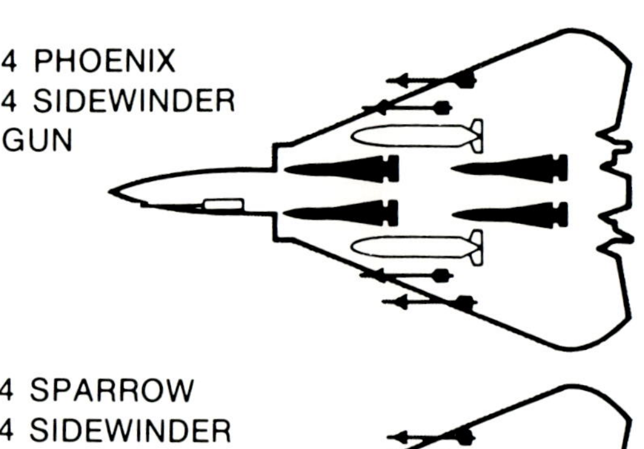

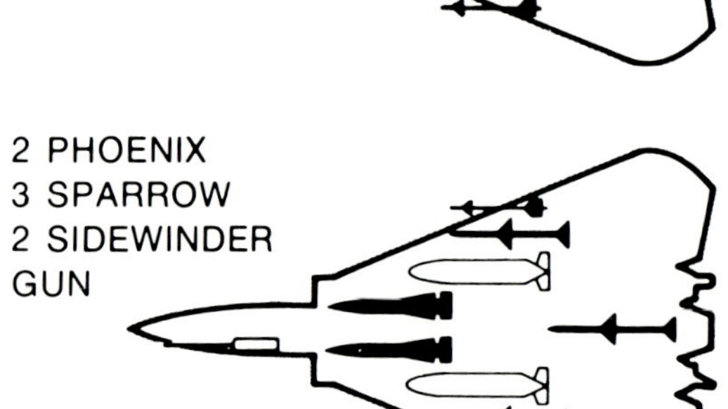

LEGEND:

SIDEWINDER MISSILE

SPARROW MISSILE

PHOENIX MISSILE

M-51 GUN

EXTERNAL FUEL TANK

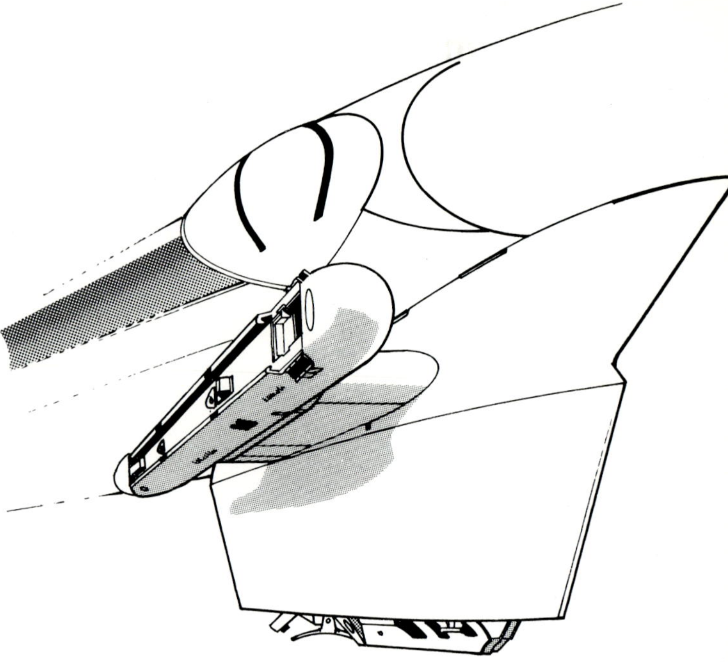

"Cranked" Pylon for Sidewinder and Sparrow Missiles

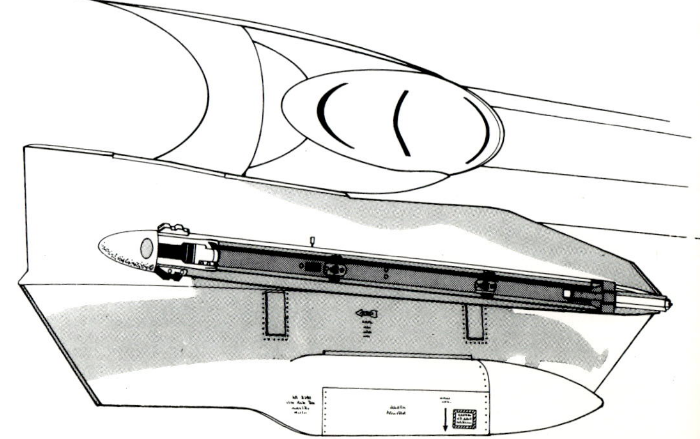

F-14A of VF-211

F-14A of VF-32

F-14A of VF-1

F-14A of VF-14, with Bicenten-
nial markings.

F-14A of VF-2 in special
three-tone gray splinter camouflage, which has been evaluated
by VF-1, 2, and VX-4. Result of
this evaluation is that all new
Tomcats for US Navy will come
out of the factory with an overall
gull gray scheme, abandoning
the practice of applying gloss
white to undersides.

First two F-14's of VF-41, over Chesapeake Bay, April, 1977. [Author]

[Above Right] Experimental "splinter" pattern camouflage was applied to some Tomcats at NAS Miramar for evaluation in ACM situations. Latest Tomcats to be delivered to the fleet will carry an overall light gull gray scheme, and official directives discourage the application of squadron markings that require large blocks of man-hours to apply and maintain. [Don Logan]

[Below Right] F-14A for the Imperial Iranian Air Force, in IIAF camouflage, with pre-delivery U.S. national insignia. Pitot tube on nose indicates that this is one of the latest [block 95] Tomcats, with automatic leading edge maneuvering slats. [Hans Redemann]

F-14A of VF-114 "Aardvarks", NAS Miramar, January, 1977. [Scott Brown]

The F-14 Weapons System…or…How to Become an Ace on the First Pass.

The AWG-9/Phoenix Missile system in the F-14 holds many world records for effectiveness. The charts below detail how the records were set. In addition to what is illustrated here, the Phoenix has demonstrated it's tenacity by achieving a kill on a QF-86 drone that had pulled 6 G's in attempting to break lock and elude the missile. The Phoenix pulled 16 G's and scored! Success rate for the first 100 Phoenix missiles fired was a phenomenal 84%! The reason for all the records, and the sub-title above, is the AWG-9 radar. It is virtually the only new thing to come along in the way of fighter radars in years. It allows the NFO to track 24 targets simultaneously, and to fire at six of them simultaneously. The AWG-9 radar covers such a great volume of airspace, compared to other sysems in contemporary service, that the F-14 crew has nearly an extra two minutes of intercept time when they spot a supersonic target.

Once fired, the Phoenix missile is on it's own. It carries it's own radar guidance system, and is capable of penetrating the most sophisticated known enemy ECM jamming screens. This allows the F-14 to maneuver against other threats. When armed with the complete mix of air-to-air weapons, (Phoenix, Sparrow, Sidewinder, and gun) the Tomcat is the most versatile and formidable fighter/interceptor you can come up against. No wonder Tomcat drivers have adopted as their standard challenge; "ANYTIME, BABY!"

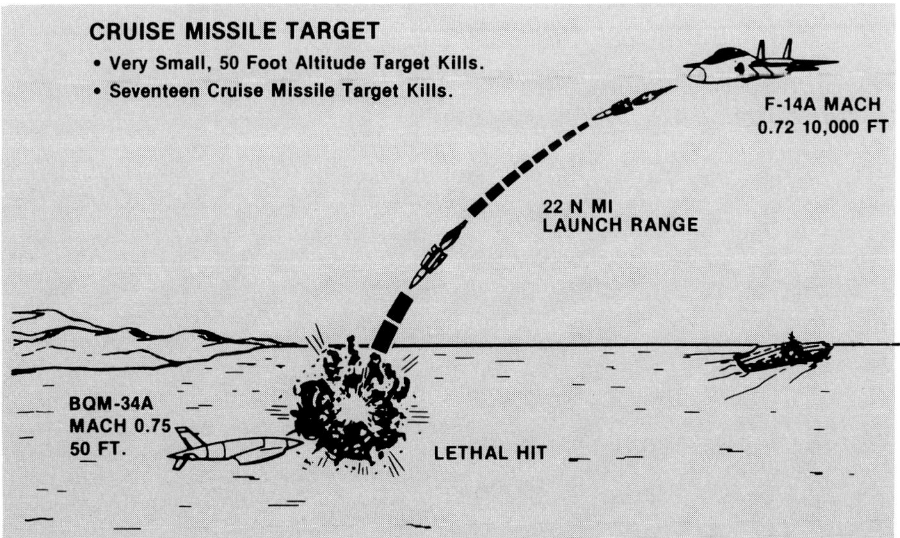

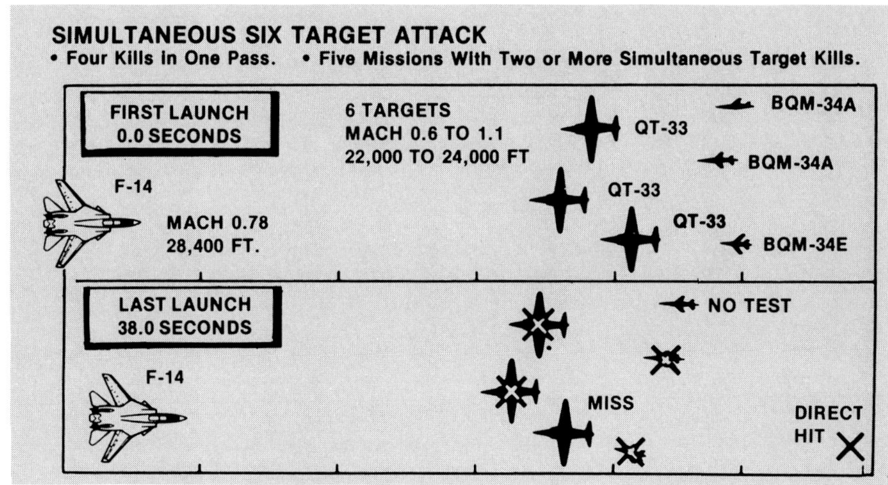

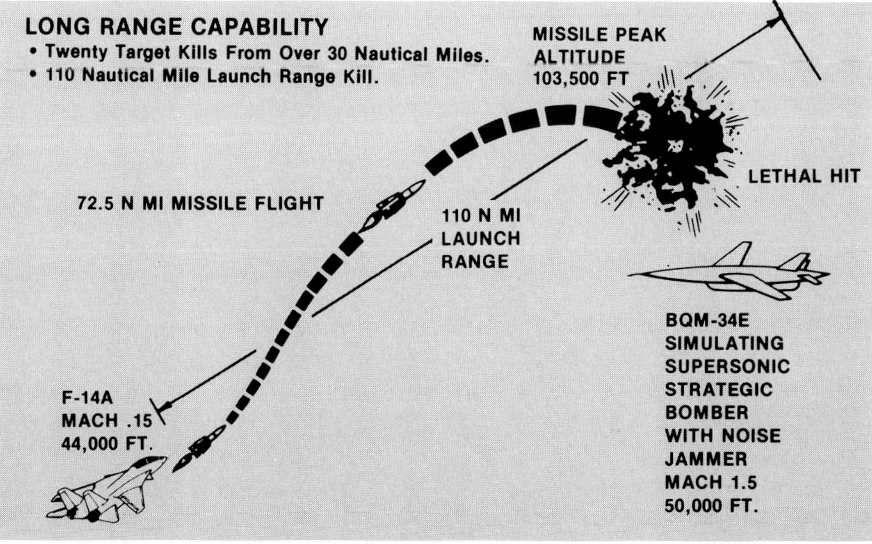

Two views of the F-14 flown by Cdr. Jim Taylor and Lt. Kurt Strauss at the 1973 Paris Air Show. Note I/R Seeker and ALQ-100 antenna under nose and the pre-production M-61 gun fairing. [Production models have a more forward enlongated gun fairing]. [Hans Redemann]

Into the Fleet

The Tomcat's official introduction to the fleet occurred on October 14, 1972, with the commissioning of the first two F-14 Squadrons, VF-1 and VF-2. Actually, neither one of these squadrons was "new" in the strictest sense of the word. In fact, they are among the oldest in the Navy.

VF-1 was originally established on July 1, 1922, and operated as such until it's redesignation to VB-2 in 1934. A year later the second VF-1 was established and served for two years, when it was redesignated VF-6. The third VF-1 was commissioned May 1, 1943, and served throughout the balance of World War II, compiling a 20 to 1 kill ratio against the Japanese. It was disestablished in October, 1945. The current VF-1 is the fourth to carry the designation, but the first "Wolfpack".

VF-2 was established at the same time as the original VF-1 and served until 1927. It was the first squadron to operate from the Navy's first carrier, the USS Langley.

The supplying of pilots constituted a heavy drain on the Officer Personnel of the Navy during the early days of Naval Aviation, and Congress decided that 30% of Naval Aviators should be enlisted men. The Navy promptly decided to form an all-enlisted fighter squadron, and VF-2 was reformed as such in January, 1927, with the original VF-2 being redesignated VF-6.

VF-2 enjoyed a varied number of assignments in the between-the-wars period, flying from NAS San Diego, various battleships, USS Langley, USS Saratoga, and USS Lexington.

When WW II broke out, most of VF-2's enlisted pilots were reassigned as instructors. The squadron fought aboard USS Lexington until she was sunk in the battle of the Coral Sea. VF-2 was disestablished on July 1, 1942. It was reformed on June 1, 1943, and compiled an enviable record against the Japanese during the march across the Pacific in 1944. The squadron was once again reformed in late 1944, and ended the war doing aerial search for POW camps in Japan. It was disestablished in November, 1945.

While the first two F-14 Squadrons were going through training with VF-124, in preparation for their first deployment, the world was introduced to the Tomcat at the Paris Air Show, in June, 1973. The professional aviation community was well aware of the controversial and turbulent developmental history of the F-14 to that date, but they were not prepared for the show that the F-14 put on at Paris.

In eight minutes of flying, a production F-14, flown by a fleet aircrew, (Cdr. Jim Taylor and Lt. Kurt Strauss, of VF-124) showed the world that the U.S. Aerospace Industry was still the world's leader in producing new generation fighter aircraft.

The flight demonstration began with a half Cuban Eight at takeoff, going through the top at 2,500 to 3,000 feet with 200 to 250 knots airspeed, followed by a slow roll, with the wings sweeping fore and aft during the maneuver. Then came a knife-edge pass at 350 to 400 knots, with a 6 G 360 degree steep turn, performed within a 2,000 foot radius at 500 feet, followed by a tuck-under break to slow to landing speed. Gear and flaps were lowered and the Tomcat

VF-124 was first squadron to operate the F-14, for the purpose of fleet squadron personnel training. Patches at right indicate willingness of Tomcat drivers to engage in ACM, and to demonstrate the superiority of their machine to all comers. Lower patch was a special run for the Paris Air Show.

performed a "wing-walking" maneuver at 105 knots down the runway, with a near vertical climb in afterburner to pattern altitude, followed by normal approach and landing.

The Paris Air Show is world-renowned for its hairy flying, with national pride on the line. Quite often, its flying demonstrations end in disaster. The Tomcat's demonstration, impressive as it was, was flown daily, and on time. The F-14's crew repeatedly stressed the fact they were not approaching the limits of the Tomcat's performance envelope, and in fact were just a fleet aircrew, flying a fleet airplane. For their performance, Cdr. Taylor and Lt. Strauss were nominated for the Harmon Trophy, which is given for outstanding aeronautical contribution in a non-combatant category. During the same show, the Russian Supersonic Transport, the TU-144, broke up in midair, crashed and burned, while attempting maneuvers outside of its performance envelope.

The F-14 went to sea for the first time, in an operational deployment, on the USS Enterprise, September 17, 1974. Ironically, it was the eighth Grumman Cat, sailing aboard the eighth ship of the line to bear the name Enterprise. It was the first Grumman fighter to be deployed since the F-11F Tiger completed it's last tour of duty in March, 1961. It was perhaps symbolic that the F-14 would, on this deployment, fly cover for the withdrawl from Vietnam in 1975....an event that was the culmination of one period in American military history, was being witnessed by a new generation of American fighter aircraft.

VF-1 flightline at NAS Miramar, late 1973. Plane captains are still in process of applying the original and distinctive "Wolfpack" markings.

Lt. Bob Vincent, of VF-1, checks Sidewinder missile during preflight of his Tomcat on first deployment of the F-14 to sea, aboard USS Enterprise. [US Navy]

With preflight complete, Vincent and his NFO prepare to mount up. [US Navy]

Vincent continues preflight with check of AIM-7 Sparrow missile. [US Navy]

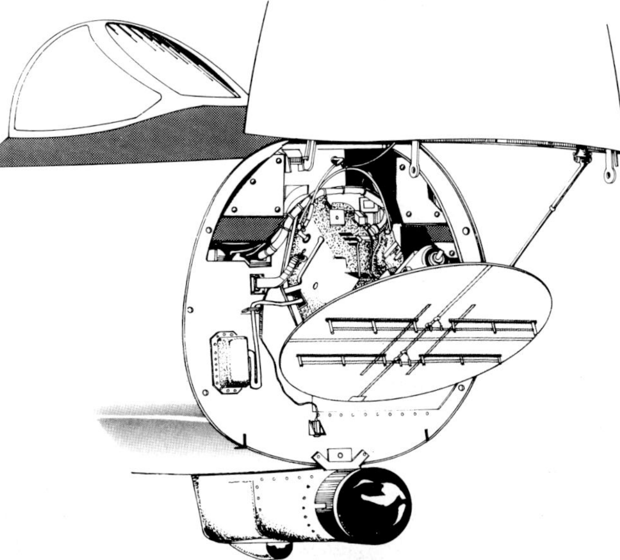

AWG-9 Radar

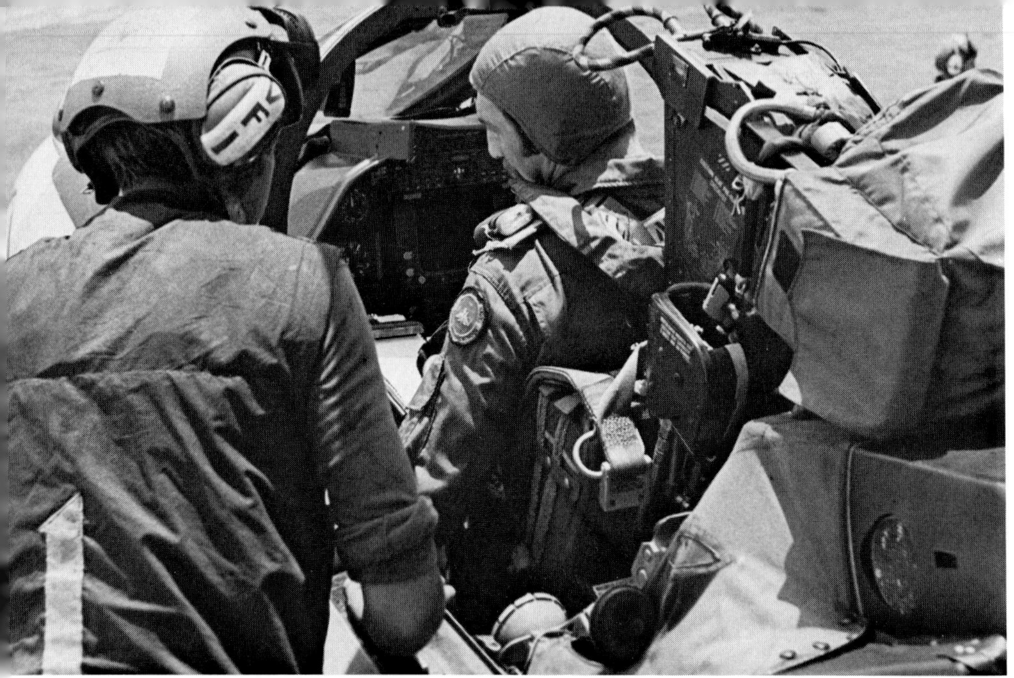

Plane Captain will assist Vincent in fastening his torso harness to parachute fittings, lap belt, and leg restraints in aircraft. Pilots often wear padded skull caps under their hard hats to reduce fatigue on long flights. [US Navy]

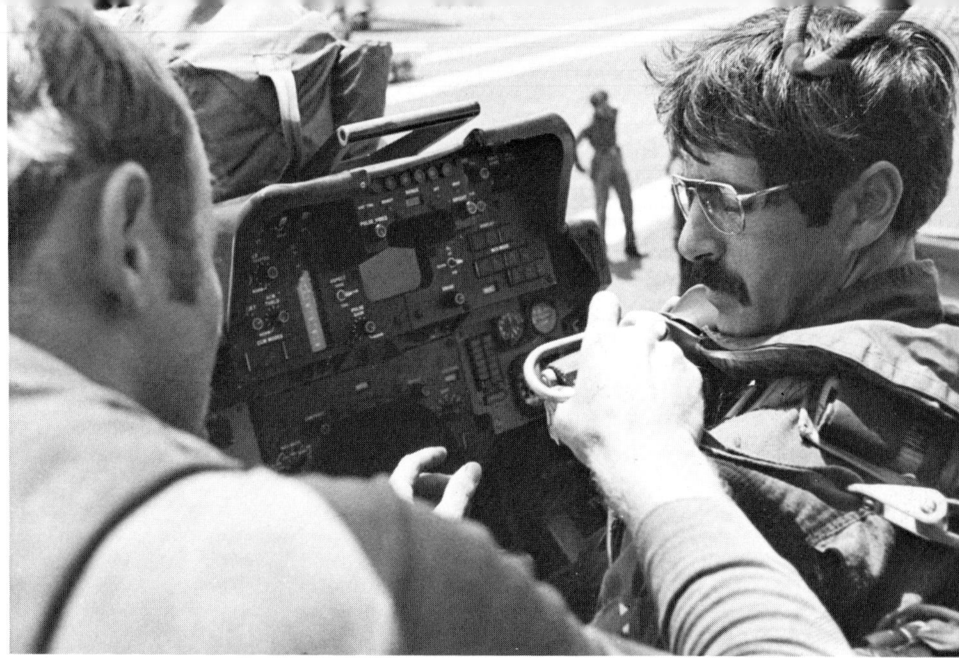

PC assists NFO in strapping into rear cockpit. [US Navy]

VF-1 crew goes through preflight checks prior to launch from USS Enterprise, March, 1974. [US Navy]

F-14 is positioned on waist cat for launch. Relatively large size of Tomcat is evident in this side-by-side comparison of Tomcat and Corsair II. [US Navy]

Seconds from completion of an "O.K. Pass", F-14 about to pounce on the number three wire of Enterprise during Westpac cruise in March of 1975. [US Navy]

Tomcat taxies forward to cat aboard Enterprise. Wings are at 75 degree oversweep used for stowage. VF-1 and VF-2 were first squadrons to take the F-14 to sea on a regular deployment, beginning in October, 1974. [US Navy]

Tomcat in landing configuration. [Bob Lawson via Jim Sullivan]

Tomcat with glove vanes extended. Glove vanes can be operated by the pilot by rotating the maneuver flap thumbwheel to the rear, up to 1.5 Mach. Above 1.5 IMN, the glove vanes are programmed full out [15 degrees] automatically by the CADC, overriding any pilot command through the thumbwheel. [US Navy]

VF-2, F-14. Antennae on fuselage spine are, from front to rear: TACAN and UHF Comm, and IFF/APX-72-UHF Data Link. Data link communications allows Tomcat crew to receive relatively jam-free real time data from Carrier Combat Information Center, or from E-2 Airborne Command Post. [US Navy]

[Left] VF-2 Tomcat is hoisted aboard USS Enterprise prior to first deployment in 1974. It carries Phoenix launch pallets on forward fuselage stations. Sparrow launch points are on fuselage centerline. [2], and under Phoenix pallets [2]. [US Navy]

VF-2 Tomcat performs low-altitude roll, while sweeping wings forward and aft, during 1976 Show at Iruma AB, Japan. [S. Ohtaki]

[Above] VF-2 Tomcat takes off from Miramar, August, 1973. [Bob Lawson via Jim Sullivan] [Right] Differential movement of stabilators is evident as Tomcat performs roll. [S. Ohtaki] [Below] 68 degree wing sweep, high speed, low altitude pass at Iruma AB, Japan. [S. Ohtaki] [Left] Postshow taxi-in at Iruma. [S. Ohtaki]

With steam from prior launch lingering, Tomcat is directed to number one cat aboard Enterprise. [US Navy]

Tomcat roars off the waist cat of Enterprise during operations in support of the evacuation of Saigon in 1975. Note stabilators in fully deflected [nose up] position. [US Navy]

Tomcat demonstrates high angle of attack climbout at Iruma. [S. Ohtaki]

Experimental camouflage applied to VF-2 Tomcat in 1976. [Don Logan]

Control Stick

[Left] VF-211 Tomcat shows off weapons load that allows maximum flexibility in air-to-air combat, including long range Phoenix, medium range Sparrow, short range Sidewinder, and, of course, real close range M-61 cannon. [Grumman] [Left Below] VF-24 "Red Checkertails" Tomcat at Miramar, January, 1976. [Bob Lawson via Jim Sullivan] [Below] VF-24 CAG aircraft tail markings consist of red check, red shadowed black "OO", and red, yellow, blue, orange, green, black, dark blue and brown stars. [clockwise from top] [Scott Brown]

F-14A of VF-211 "Checkmates" at NAS Miramar, May, 1976. Open access door on fuselage ahead of ventral fins is engine oil refill point. [Duane Kasulka via Jim Sullivan]

Flight of VF-211 Tomcats over California desert. [Grumman]

VF-213 Tomcats sport medium blue tail markings, with yellow stars, twin tailed [Naturally!] Black Lion with yellow mane [squadron namesake]. [Scott Brown]

F-14's of VF-114. These are all block ninety-five airplanes, and are configured for Sparrow Missiles on fuselage, and two Sidewinders on each of the pylons. "Boattail" between exhausts is tipped with navigation light [white], and fuel dump mast. Light area on vertical fin tips [outboard both sides] is low light level formation light, which are also carried on fuselage, just ahead of turbine warning stripe, above "NAVY", and on nose, just above M-61 cannon fairing. These lights are now common to most fighter aircraft of both services. [Scott Brown]

A Tale of Two Tails…or… I Fly the Tomcat

F-14A of VF-101 "Grim Reapers" approaching NAS Oceana for landing. VF-101 was the first East Coast Tomcat Squadron, and serves as the Atlantic Fleet replacement training component on the F-14. [Jim Sullivan]

You're too slow! Too much sink! Pullup! Pullup! Too late, I hauled back on the stick and added power. Then, everything stopped. I had just augered in the F-14. But what followed was not a journey through diaphanous mists to the great beyond. Instead a voice sounded in my headset: "Open the canopy Lou, and let someone else have a go at it." More than a little sheepishly, I popped the canopy of the F-14, and looked up at Lt. Dave Davis, who was grinning down at me from the platform of the F-14 simulator room at NAS Oceana. I had just spent a half an hour trying to fly the best fighter that has ever been built, and I had made a Walter Mitty-shattering discovery. Seven hundred hours in assorted lightplanes does not a fighter pilot make. I hoped I would do better from the back seat, because tommorrow I was going to be flying the real thing, and the F-14 is definitely a two man airplane. (You can't get the Tomcat out of the chocks without the Naval Flight Officer who sits behind the pilot.)

Earlier in the day I had spent an hour and a half in the rear seat simulator, learning the position of switches, and the proper sequence in which to punch them. That time, coupled with some intense cramming with the manual whenever I got the chance, would suffice to get us airborne. But all that encompassed was turning on the radios, completing the on-board-checks, and alignment of the inertial navigation system. We hardly even scratched the surface when it came to operating the complex weapons system of the F-14. And that weapons system is at the heart of the Tomcat's undisputed (in my eyes) title "Champion Fighter Of All Time". The well-trained NFO is more than just another set of eyes in the F-14. He is half of the team that makes the Tomcat what it is, and the Navy is completely sold on the two-man fighter concept.

Briefing for the flight was scheduled for 1045. I arrived an hour early. (More study of the large chart containing the rear seat panel and consoles.) The troops at VF-101's F-14 component were enthusiastic about making a new convert to the Tomcat fan club, and they kept telling me how much I was going to enjoy myself on the hop. My anticipation matched their enthusiasm, and since they are all experienced fighter pilots, with time in every fighter the Navy has operated in the past decade, I was prepared to be impressed.

Lt. Joe Reeves was my pilot. We would be leading a two plane section. Piloting the other F-14 was Capt. "Jammer" Afshar, of the Imperial Iranian Air Force. VF-101 is tasked with training many of the Iranian pilots who will return to Iran as instructors on their new Tomcats. This was to be Afshar's third hop in the F-14, and his first formation flight. The Iranians now going through the F-14 sylabbus are some of the best in the Shah's Air Force, with hundreds of hours in the F-4. Afshar's NFO was Lt. Barry Recame, also a VF-101 instructor.

Lt. Reeves conducted the briefing, which consisted in the main of formation flying techniques in the F-14. He told Afshar to use the ejection seat warning triangle below the rear cockpit as a visual cue, keeping it just under the leading edge of the intake to maintain the proper formation position. He also warned Afshar about getting "sucked in" by the lead F-14's bow wave. If that happens, he said, don't try to slide out by lifting a wing, as you will only stick your wing into my belly. Put the nose down, get some vertical separation, then use rudder to slide out. He went through hand signals used to command "gear down", "flaps down", "speed brakes out", then explained the F-14's characteristics in that configuration. He completed the briefing with the smilingly uttered admonishment: "Fly safe, Jammer! I've never had a midair yet!" (I heartily concurred with his sentiments.)

Dressing for the role of a fighter pilot is an experience no pilot should be denied. In my case, it was like putting black stripes on a yellow housecat. First the G suit wraps around your waist, zipping up the side, then you hold your breath, bend down, and zip the leggings up the inseam of your legs. (Experienced fighter pilots can actually carry on a conversation while doing this…me, I felt like Clark Kent, and I couldn't imagine him talking to Lois Lane while he got his fighter pilot suit on.) Next, you step into the torso harness, which will act as your parachute harness, should the need arise. (Koch fittings on the harness snap to seat belt and parachute risers in the airplane.) Now you strap leg restraints on your calves. They will snap to fittings on the seat, which will yank your legs back tight against the seat during the ejection sequence. This will ensure you of taking your legs with you if you eject. Finally, you are ready to shrug into, zip up, and snap together your survival vest, which contains such goodies as flare gun, knife, strobe light, water bottle, riser cutters, survival radio, and combination flare and smoke signal. Helmet in hand, knee board under arm, and we are ready to head for the airplane.

Much of what happens on a fighter flightline is performed by rote. The obvious reasons for this are the fact that it is too noisy to be doing a lot of talking, and if you don't know your job well enough to perform it with a minimum of conversation, you probably won't be on the flightline long anyway. We put our helmets on before the walk out to the airplane, so I was able to drink in and savor this moment in the sun. It was a gorgeous day, and I was a participant, rather than spectator, for a change.

While Joe Reeves performed his walkaround, I climbed into the rear seat. The plane captain followed me up the ladder, and assisted me in finding and fastening all of the straps. Lap belt, parachute risers, leg restraints, oxygen mask, G suit, and communications cord were all in place. Joe leaned into the rear cockpit to tell me to arm the ejection seat. There are two methods of firing the ejection seat, and both of them must be armed before you can use the seat. Since the seat has zero airspeed and zero altitude capability, it is armed before you start. The firing handle between your legs has a safety lever that must be rotated to your left and down, and the face curtain handles are armed with a smaller lever behind and over your head.

Now that I was settled into the cockpit, I began to look for a place to put my camera so that I could use both hands to perform my duties in getting us underway. The cockpit of a fighter is a functional place, and there is not a lot of room for extraneous materials. I finally found a spot at the far left rear corner of the cockpit, on the left console.

While Joe was strapping in, I began to check switch positions. Let's see now, start on the left console. Radio is off, TACAN is off, AWG-9 liquid cooling switch is off. Now on to the panel...Ground test panel is covered, Nav mode switch is off, AWG-9 power...hmmmm...oh yeah, that's right in front of the radar control handle...o.k. that's off, and the IFF...(transponder to you civilians)...got to reach to the right and back to get that one, and it's off."

Joe is in now, and comes up on the intercom. "How do you read me, Lou?" I punch the ICS (Inter Com Switch) button on the floor with my left foot. "Loud and clear." O.K., canopy is coming closed...keep clear of the rails." The canopy hisses down into place. I glanced over in time to see it slam forward the last couple of inches, locking into place.

You might think that things would quiet down considerably with the outside world now shut out by plexiglas. Not so. The F-14 cockpit is a relatively noisy place, though not uncomfortably so, and I have to think that there is a measure of security in being able to hear and judge engine noise.

Joe is on the ICS again, telling me that he is starting the engines. There is a series of hissing noises, and the cockpit begins to pressurize. My ears begin to tell me things are happening, and I'm glad I don't have the mask on yet...I can still yawn to clear them. The plane captain is stationed opposite the front cockpit, and he signals as various stages of the start procedure progress. With both engines running, Joe does his check of the emergency generator. His notification that the check is complete is my signal to spring into action. It is time for my sole mandatory contribution to the flight.

I reach to my left on the console and push the eject command lever forward to the "pilot" position. (If that decision has to be made, it won't be me that's making it!) Now the AWG-9 liquid cooling switch to the rear, while the AWG-9 power switch is pushed forward to the "stand-by" position. TACAN and Radio are both on the left console, and they are switched on. The IFF is on the right, and it is put in the stand-by position. Now for the On Board Checks (OBC). Joe comes on the ICS to tell me he has selected OBC, and I can proceed with the On Board Checks. I rotate the category knob on the console-mounted keyboard to "Special", then punch the OBC bit button. Instantly the radar screen in front

Tomcat Mechanic's Patch

of me comes alive with a column of four acronyms as the computer interrogates the systems and checks on their well-being. (Any faults it finds are reported below the four columns of acronyms.) With the OBC test complete, I check the altimeter for the correct setting. Now for the alignment of the inertial navigation system.

I reach up and switch the Nav Mode to "ground", then turn the category switch on the keyboard panel to "Nav". Consulting the alignment card on my kneeboard, I punch in LAT (Latitude), N&E, 3, 6, 4, 8, 9. It appears on the Tactical Information Display (TID-radar screen) in front of me. Assured that I have the correct information selected, I punch the "ENTER" buttom. Next I punch LONG (Longitude), E & W, 7, 6, 0, 2, 1, check the printout for accuracy, and again hit the "ENTER" button. The Tactical Information Display screen in front of me now has three short vertical lines dividing the bottom third of the screen. Within 20 seconds a check mark appears at the extreme left of the screen, and begins to move across the screen. At this point, three lights are lit on the panel. The "NAV COMP" on the right knee panel, and the "STBY" and "READY" lights on the upper left corner of the TID panel. As th alignment of the Inertial Navigation System (INS) continues, they will extinguish to indicate progress towards full readiness of the system. On the TID the check mark passes the first vertical line at two and a half minutes into the alignment, and turns into a diamond. This indicates alignment with degraded accuracy, and is accompanied by the "NAV COMP" light going out. At four minutes into the alignment, the diamond has progressed past the second vertical mark, and we would now be able to leave the line assured to accuracy to within 4.5 nautical miles in an hour. The final fine honing of the system takes another two and a half minutes, and gives us accuracy to within .75 nautical miles in an hour.

At this point, a real NFO would enter his waypoint data, perform the TACAN BIT, then switch the NAV MODE to INS. Since I am about six months short of NFO training, I content myself with performing the last function. The INS will now give us continuous readouts on our position as the flight progresses.

With alignment of the INS complete, Joe comes on the ICS to tell me that we can complete the BIT checks. Our wingman has boarded ten minutes after us, and I'm thankful that I have plenty of time to consult the checklists on my kneeboard. I rotate the category button back to "BIT", and punch the upper left button on the keyboard. A little green arrow appears to let me know I have punched it, and the TID displays a box in the upper center of the screen. When

Tomcats of VF-14 "Tophatters". In photo at left, inlet bleed air doors are prominently displayed on top of wing glove, just behind ECS heat exchanger outlets. [darker areas] Note single walk area painted on top of port intake. Tomcat above has Phoenix pylon under wing glove area, and carries special multi-purpose pallets under fuselage. [US Navy & Bob Lawson via Jim Sullivan]

a check mark appears in the lower left corner of the box, I will know that BIT 1 is complete. If any discrepancies are found, the computer will print them out on the bottom of the screen. (The crew will now know if they have to fly the mission with a degraded system, and which parts of the system are inoperative.) We complete BIT 1 and BIT 2 in the chocks. BIT 3 involves turning the radar transmitter on, and since it's transmissions could be harmful to any ground crewmen standing in front of the airplane, it is usually done while taxiing to the runway.

With the checks complete, Joe gives a thumbs up to the plane captain, and he waves us out of our parking spot. We taxi to the end of the line, stop, and Joe "kneels" the airplane down for final checks by the ground crew. (In this respect the F-14 is just the opposite of the F-4. Whereas, with the F-4 the nose is raised for a cat shot to give maximum angle of attack...and attain max lift at the end of the cat...the Tomcat's nose is depressed so that the catapult launch bar can be attached to the catapult shuttle.) The ground crewmen perform final checks, and with a smart salute, we are waved onto the taxiway.

The Tomcat is like other carrier aircraft I have ridden in on the ground. It rides hard. Each bump and crack in the pavement is telegraphed right to the seat of your pants, and I can see how the landing gear would survive 25 foot per second smashes onto the deck. (This is not the normal rate of descent, but it is what the Navy had specified for the gear, and during testing the gear proved tougher than the test pilot who was testing it and put himself into the hospital with a severe back compression.)

Approaching the end of runway 32, we swing around to runway heading for final checks. I ask Joe if he wants me to read the checklist. He replies that he will read it aloud, both challenge and response, and the following litany comes over the ICS; "Brakes...Brakes OK, accumulator pressure up. Fuel...normal feed auto trans...dumps off...16,000 pounds showing on the counter...exterior trans checked. Canopy...handle closed, hooks engaged...lines check OK, light out. Seat...armed forward, pilot in window...is your command lever forward? "right"...OK...SAS switches, all on...all circuit breakers in...master test, off. Bi-directional pump...normal. Compass and standby gyro, compass synced,

standby gyro erect." I watch a couple of A-6's in the touch and go pattern come in, touch down, then rotate into the air again immediately. Two F-4's from VF-11 pull up next to us to do their preflight checks. Finally our wingman taxies into position for his last minute checks. The tower clears our flight...Gunfighter 153 and 174 into position on the runway.

A nudge of the throttles, engage nosewheel steering, push the rudder pedal, and we bump onto the runway, lining up to the right of the centerline. Our wingman follows, lining up to the left and behind us. Time now for the final pre-takeoff checks, and Joe is on the ICS again; "Wings, 20 degrees, auto both lights out...check them visually...and...they are at 20 degrees. Flaps and slats indicate down, and they are. Spoilers, outboard spoiler mod...on...speed brake...select spoilers up...check them...and they are up...speed brake off. Check trim neutral...harness locked...got your's locked? "right". Check controls...OK...check warning lights all out...are your's all out? "right"...O.K. Lou, we're ready to roll, and as soon as we get a thumbs up from Jammer, we'll be rolling."

We are both looking over our left shoulders now, watching for the thumbs up that will indicate that our wingman is ready to follow us. When it comes, Joe sets the brakes, goes to zone two afterburner, then releases the brakes.

The F-14 leaps forward, then Joe goes to zone five afterburner, and there is another slam in the back. I have never felt this kind of acceleration in an airplane. Experimentally, I try to lean forward into it. I can't! Somewhat sheepishly, I remember that my harness is locked. Still, I doubt that you could overcome the inertia being generated by better than 40,000 pounds of thrust from those twin TF-30s behind us. I dart a quick look at the airspeed...better than 100 knots already! The needle seems to surge through 120 knots, and we are airborne. Less than 1500 feet of runway are behind us, and we are climbing rapidly. Gear is up, then in seconds, we are level at 1,000 feet, and the flaps are coming up. Joe banks left, and I look back to see Jammer cutting inside to join up.

Steady now on course 160, we have gotten departure control clearance for a Tidewater one departure. Afshar is tucked in on our right wing, and I am

F-14s of VF-32 fly formation on E-2C Hawkeye of VAW-125. Tomcat and Hawkeye operating as a unit gives the fleet unparalleled defensive capability, as their highly advanced radar systems complement each other. With the F-14 operating on the outer edge of the defensive perimeter, its radar can be shut down and, through the use of data-link with the E-2C, it can be vectored into position for intercepts. With it's radar shut down, the F-14 is more difficult to track, and can avoid radar emissions seeking missiles fired by enemy aircraft. [US Navy]

beginning to appreciate two highly touted features of the Tomcat. The visibility is great out of the bubble canopy, and it is a comfortable airplane. (In the Phantom I would already be fidgeting around, trying to find a more comfortable position.) Center has cleared us to 15,000, and as we level off, Barry calls for handoff to Longshot Control. Longshot is the local controller who will oversee activities in the restricted airspace alloted to the military. Barry calls Longshot to advise them of our intended activities, and they let us know that there is ACM activity in the southern sector. Barry rogers and tells them we will stay north. Afshar has stayed glued to our wing throughout, and from what I can see, he is doing a great job. Joe calls; "Gunfighter 174, slide in a little so you can get a taste of that bow wave I was telling you about." Jammer begins to disappear behind our starboard intake, and I begin to fidget...suddenly, he pops back out...lower, and farther behind. Barry calls; "He handled it well, Joe." Now we will separate to give Afshar a chance at some join-ups.

Joe banks left, and pulls...and suddenly, I feel the G suit squeezing. "How many G's was that Joe?..."Oh, about two and a half...maybe three." It felt like four or five, I'm thinking to myself, and I resolve to tighten up a little on the next one. We've got about two or three miles separation now, and Joe rolls out and looks back. Afshar is coming up on the left side, but to Joe's practiced eye, he is too far back. "He's too far back...sucked out...there...that's better." Gunfighter 174 slides in on the port side. Joe calls; "OK 174, let's try one to the right." The horizon tilts 90 degrees and we pull around to the right. This time I'm ready, and the G's are more comfortable. Looking back to the right, we can see 174 well out to the side and cutting our circle nicely. A much better join-up this time, and Joe is satisfied with Jammer's performance to the right, but wants to try another to the left. We bank hard left again, and I'm really starting to enjoy the responsiveness of the Tomcat. There is just something about the way a fighter handles...you can feel the power...and I am struck again by the feeling of limitless freedom...but the best is yet to come. After Afshar joins up, we go through cycling the gear, flaps, and speed brakes down. 174

maintains his relative position throughout, and I am impressed. Either the soft-spoken Iranian is a hell of a pilot, (remember, this is only his third hop in the F-14, and his first formation flight) or the F-14 is a pussycat to fly in formation. (After my experience in the simulator, I would prefer to believe the former.)

Satisfied that we have accomplished the formation training portion of our mission, Joe calls Longshot Control to ask if they have contact with "Fast Eagle". Fast Eagle is a flight of two F-14's from VF-41. They are brand new block ninety five Tomcats, the first 2 airplanes the Black Aces have received, and they have agreed to fly formation on us for the benefit of my camera. The Fast Eagles are not up yet, so Joe shows me some of the Tomcat's Air Combat Maneuvering (ACM) capabilities by pulling away from Afshar, then rolling up and over our wingman. If it were not for the obvious energy involved, (which I am acutely aware of, since I cannot raise my camera to eye level during these maneuvers) the ease with which the F-14 eats up airspace...up, down, and laterally...would seem to belie the skill demanded of today's fighter pilot. But the F-14 has crossed a technological threshold, not only in terms of it's "magic" weapons systems, but perhaps more importantly...in the eyes of the fighter pilot...aerodynamically. I have experienced the forces generated by high energy fighter aircraft before...in the F-4, and F-101. I am about to experience the qualities that make the Tomcat truly unique.

We are straight and level at 15,000 feet, indicating 375 knots. Joe warns me to straighten up, to avoid discomfort in the forthcoming maneuver. Then he tells me to imagine that we have somebody at our six, about to start shooting at us. Then...well, if I didn't know better, I would swear he had ejected me! I am crushed...smashed...by an instant 6.5 Gs! I am sure my back is broken. (It's not, and there is no aftereffect) What we have done is to turn the closest thing to a square corner that is possible in an airplane. Joe had pulled the stick...really snatched it...straight back. We have lost two hundred knots of airspeed, and are going almost straight up. He rolls 180 degrees, pulls down behind our "enemy", and rolls out. Now, there are two things about this maneuver that are really impressive (other than the fact that I survived it). First of all, the Tomcat did not depart controlled flight, which is probably something no other airplane could achieve. Secondly, in the blink of an eye, we have gone from defense to offense.

Having demonstrated one method of shaking a potential threat, Joe climbs to 20,000 feet to demonstrate the docility of this latest Grumman cat. Level at 20,000 in military power, he comes back on the stick smoothly until we have achieved 85 degrees of pitch up. The climb is impressive at first, pegging the rate of climb at 6,000 feet per minute. Then, as our energy is dissipated, the rate of climb sags, and the airspeed goes with it...down...down...through the advertised "stall speed" of 103 knots...and beyond...to zero! It feels as though we have defeated gravity, and are literally hanging suspended in the air with our nose pointed almost straight up. But gravity is an adversary that cannot be fooled. We are now sliding back down, at the rate of 9,000 feet per minute. Unlike any airplane that I have ever flown, there is no buffet, no abrupt, nose slashing pitch down. Instead, the Tomcat lazily, ever so gently, points it's nose slowwwwwwly towards the horizon, picking up speed as it goes, as if it were alive and searching for the airspeed needed to negate that horrendous 9,000 foot-per-minute fall. Throughout this maneuver, it remains the epitome of constraint, refusing to exhibit the nasty tendencies many of it's

Tomcat of VF-142 "Ghostriders" refuelling from KA-6 Tanker of VA-176 over the Mediterranean. USS America steams in the background. During 1976 deployment, VF-142 averaged 16 sorties per day, each of approximately two hours duration. [US Navy]

VF-142 Tomcat, with Sparrow and Sidewinder launch rails under wing glove. [Bruce Trombecky via Jim Sullivan]

One of the most dramatic moments in Naval Aviation... night launch! [US Navy]

Prototype Infared Sensor

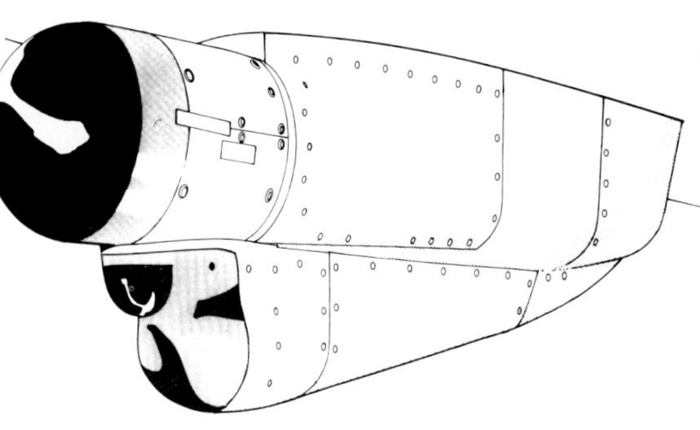

ALQ-100 Antenna

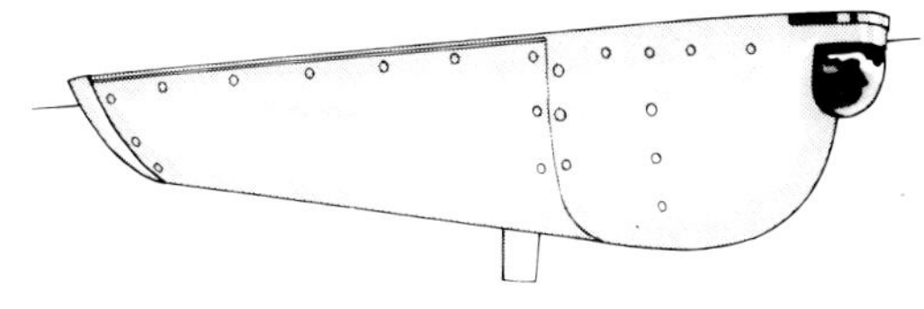

VF-143 "Pukin' Dogs" Tomcat leaves the waist cat of USS American during 1976 Mediterranean Sea cruise. F-14s speed at end of catapult is 145 knots. [US Navy]

VF-143 Tomcats with wings fully forward. Sweep angles of 20 degrees through 75 degrees result in wing span variation of 33 to 64 feet. [US Navy]

contemporaries would throw at you, such as a spin. Not only has the airframe behaved in an exemplary manner, but the turbofan engines have refused to stall to boot! Just to prove that there was nothing extraordinary about this maneuver, (for the Tomcat) Joe repeats it, with one exception. This time he saves enough travel on the stick to give a healthy yank rearward as we approach zero airspeed.

The result is practically the same, except that the pitch down is slightly more pronounced. The nose goes straight down...ninety degrees...and as soon as we have airspeed, he pulls out. This is one behavioral aspect of the F-14 that was not anticipated by Grumman, and is the apparent result of the wide, flat fuselage acting as a lifting body. This inherent honesty, coupled with automatic wing sweep scheduling and the heads-up display, makes the F-14 the best dogfighting, air superiority fighter ever built. Throw in the NFO

with the AWG-9 weapons system and Phoenix Missiles, and you have the best interceptor ever built. So what we have here is the best pure air fighting machine ever. And it is being improved during production.

Block ninety and upward F-14's will have automatic leading edge maneuvering slats, a new central air data computer, and a new UHF radio. The maneuvering slats are programmed to pop out at 13 units angle of attack, and retract at 11 units AOA. The slats have solved one annoying characteristic of the Tomcat, which was demonstrated to me. At 12 to 14 units AOA, there is the onset of buffet, which remains until you ease off to lower AOA. Looking in the mirror during this maneuver, I was horrified to see the twin tails wagging like a happy dog's. The buffet does not signify the onset of any drastic or unplanned maneuver though, and the AOA can be flown right up to 30 units. Installation of the automatic slats though, has resulted in an increase of ½ to 1 more "G" in sustained turning performance.

It doesn't take much imagination to figure out what this means to the young, low time fighter pilot. He can now reach for that ragged edge that is required to turn ordinary fighter pilots into world-beaters, and do so with more confidence. It means that the U.S. Navy will have a fighter force that is second to none in the world, and cost and time required to train that force is drastically cut.

Our rendezvous with Fast Eagle for picture taking seems sort of anticlimactic now...except that I am now more impressed than ever with the breathtaking beauty of these two sleek juggernauts as we dart from right to left, over and under them while I snap away the film. One pass over Oceana with VF-41's Tomcats in tight, wings-fully-swept-formation, and we break off to enter the pattern.

If there is one maneuver universally enjoyed by all fighter pilots and would-be fighter pilots, (I do it all the time in my T-34) it is the break from initial to downwind leg of the traffic pattern. We roared down the duty runway at 300 knots, 800 feet above the runway, then Joe cranked into a 60 degree screaming bank to the left. He switched to hot mike and read the checklist as he acomplished each of the items: "Wings...20 degrees, auto...Wheels...three down...Flaps...full down...Hook...is up...Harness...locked...got your's locked? "Rog"...Good...O.K....Speed brakes...out".

At the 180 degree abeam position he has the airplane trimmed at 15 units AOA. DLC and APC (Direct Lift Control and Approach Power Compensator) are on. I am surprised at how tight the pattern appears to be...I have séen a lot of guys fly wider patterns in their 172's, but then the Navy does not like to dawdle around when recovering aircraft aboard ship, and I guess that Navy pilots are taught to get it on right now. I have also seen guys louse up a landing that they have worked on for five minutes. We rolled out on final with an "on speed" approach indexer indication, and maintained our 15 units right down to the deck. As soon as the main gear struts compressed, Joe pushed the throttles forward to mil power, and we leapt off in runway on our go-around. No matter how many fighter types I fly in, I am always most impressed with the excess power. We got to pattern altitude in what seemed like milli-seconds, turned crosswind, then downwind, and re-read the checklist. The second landing was full-stop, and as smooth as a carrier landing could possibly be. It's all over now, except for the taxi back to our parking spot, and I am saddened. But I am also a man with a mission. I have become a certified convert. The Tomcat is everything they told me it would be, and then some!

[Left & Center Left] VF-84 "Jolly Rogers" Tomcat is one of the new block 95 airplanes. DECM RCVR antenna is carried on tip of starboard vertical fin. Area of tailpipes varies from 7.5 square feet full open [shown here], and 3.53 feet in closed position. Tailpipe nozzels are infinitely variable between these positions, and open and close automatically in response to amount of thrust being generated by the engines. [Jim Sullivan]

[Below Left] VF-84 will take it's Tomcats to sea on USS Nimitz. [Tom Hayden]

VF-41 crew straps into one of their brand-new block 95 Tomcats, NAS Oceana, April, 1977. [Author]

VF-41 has the only black-nosed Tomcats in the fleet. Black nose is a tradition with "Black Aces" fighters. Factory-fresh gull-grey finish on these Tomcats had a distinctive sheen to it. [Author]

DECM High Band antenna is contained in the boattail, next to fuel dump mast. [above] [Jim Sullivan] VF-41 will operate from USS Nimitz when they go to sea.

46

VX-4 operates several Tomcats from their base at PMTC, Point Mugu, California. They are tasked with determining the full potential of the F-14 in the air superiority role [above] [Dr. C. Eddy via Norm Taylor]

Large bubble canopy of the Tomcat provides it's crew with first pre-requisite of the air-superiority machine...superior vision. [US Navy]

Latest version of the Tomcat formates on the number three airplane, which carries a pair of practice AIM-9 missiles. [Grumman]

Grumman's F-14 assembly line at Calverton. New Tomcats for Navy and Imperial Iranian Air Force are being completed. Iran will take delivery of 80 F-14s. [left] Completed Iranian Tomcat awaits delivery at Grumman plant. [below] First Tomcats were delivered to Iran on January 30, 1976. They are being produced at the rate of two per month. [Hans Redemann]

View of the F-14 that potential aggressor might expect to find in his rear-view mirror. The Tomcat is the first of the new generation of U.S. fighters, and it is as dominant in the worldwide fighter scenario as any of it's predecessors in the famed Grumman "Iron Works" stable.

SS1036 F6F Hellcat in Action

SS1045 P-51 Mustang in Action

SS1067 P-47 Thunderbolt in Action

squadron/signal publications presents

THE MAGNIFICENT SEVEN!

SS1044 Messerschmitt Bf109 in Action Part 1
SS1057 Messerschmitt Bf109 in Action Part 2

SS1039 Spitfire in Action

SS1029 F4U Corsair in Action

SS1059 A6M Zero in Action